DISCARDED

The collector's all-colour guide to

Transport

TOYS

An international survey of tinplate and diecast commercial
vehicles from 1900 to the present day

The collector's all-colour guide to
Transport
TOYS

An international survey of tinplate and diecast commercial
vehicles from 1900 to the present day

Gordon Gardiner & Richard O'Neill

**TIGER BOOKS INTERNATIONAL
LONDON**

A Salamander Book

Acknowledgements

This edition published in 1989 by
Tiger Books International PLC, London.

Reprinted in 1990

© Salamander Books Ltd 1985

ISBN 1 85501 026 7

Designer:
Barry Savage

Photography:
Terry Dilliway
© Salamander Books Ltd.

Filmset:
Modern Text Typesetting Ltd.

Colour reproduction:
Melbourne Graphics

Printed in Belgium.

In the preparation of this book we received the most generous assistance and advice
from many toy collectors. Without the help of the individuals listed below, this record
of the transport toys of the 20th century could not have been assembled.

Geoffrey Baker,
Liss, Hampshire

Glen Butler,
Henfield, Sussex

David Chester,
Bognor Regis, Sussex

John Churchward,
London
Pages: 32-33; 44-45; 46-47; 48-49; 56-57; 58-59; 60-61; 114-115; 116-117

Chris Littledale,
The British Engineerium Museum, Hove, Sussex

Shaun Magee Pedal Car Collection,
Bishop's Waltham, Hampshire

Ken McCrae,
London

Ron McCrindell,
Sidmouth, Devon

Peter Moore,
Motor Book Postal Auctions, West Chiltington, Sussex

Clive Willoughby,
London

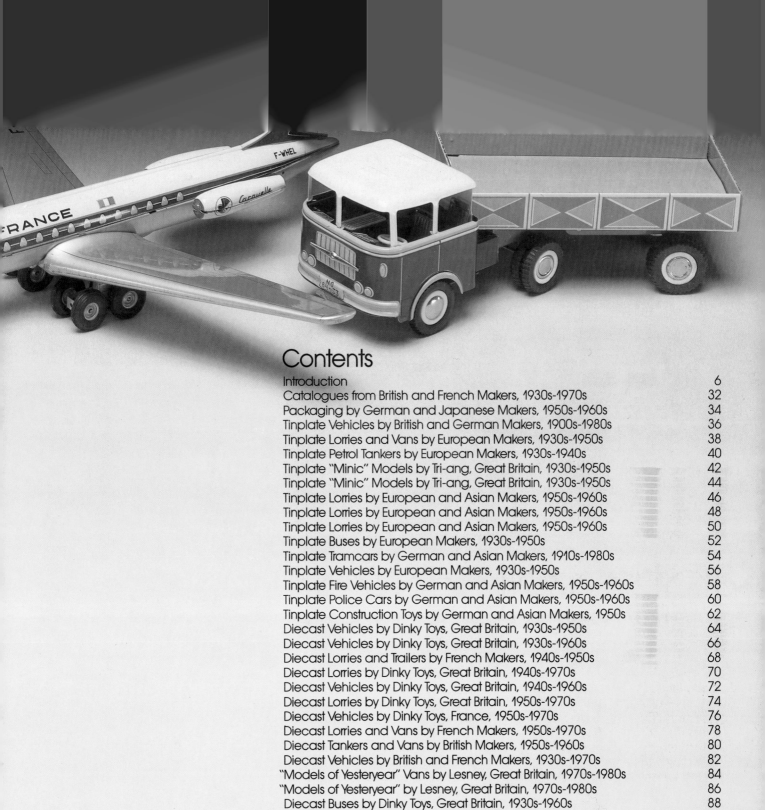

Contents

Introduction

As was the case with our companion volume, "Toy Cars", it is most appropriate that this book should appear in 1985, the year which, it is generally agreed, marks the centenary of the motor vehicle as we know it; that is, a road vehicle powered by a petrol-driven internal combustion engine.

Toymakers were quick to take advantage of the fascination exerted by mechanical transport over so many of their potential customers: a fascination that extended far beyond the ranks of those who could, in the earlier period of the automotive industry, ever hope to own a real vehicle, and one that embraced adults and children alike. By the beginning of the 20th century, metal and wooden toys representing road transport vehicles (and, of course cars, which are dealt with in our companion volume referred to above) of all kinds were appearing in sizes ranging from diminutive tinplate "penny toys" (intended to sell for about that sum or its local equivalent) to pedal-powered models (usually made of wood in the earlier days) large enough to accommodate a juvenile driver and sometimes a passenger as well.

SCOPE OF THE BOOK

Both of the present authors were concerned, one as co-author and the other as editor, in the production of an earlier Salamander publication, "The All-Colour Directory of Metal Toys" by Gordon Gardiner and Alistair Morris, which appeared in 1984. In that book, the "classic" tinplate vehicles (ie, those produced between c1900 and World War I, and, to a lesser extent, between c1920 and 1939) by such toymakers as Bing, Carette, Günthermann, Märklin, and, from a slightly later period, Citroën, CIJ, Jep, Kingsbury and others, were well represented

We wished to avoid as far as possible the duplication of material that we had already presented to the reader in "Metal Toys", and in this book coverage of the tinplate toys of the earlier classic period is limited to the vehicles shown on *pages 34-35*, the toy boats on *pages 108-109* and the boats and aircraft on *pages 110-111* (the toys on all these pages coming from the internationally-famous collection of Ron McCrindell, the doyen of British toy collectors and a major source of help to us in the compilation of this and

earlier books). However, a fair number of tinplate toys of the later classic period, up to World War II, are shown—vehicles on *pages 36-37, 50-51* and *52-53;* aeroplanes on *pages 110-111* and *112-113*—and we have included a wide selection of tinplate transport toys made since World War II: *pages 38-39, 44-45, 46-47, 48-49, 54-55, 56-57, 58-59, 60-61, 114-115* and *116-117*. Among the latter are many examples of the increasingly-collectable tinplate toys made in the 1950s-1970s by Japanese and other Far Eastern makers; these were most kindly made available to us by the noted London collector and dealer John Churchward.

MODERN PRICES

However, a strong argument against the inclusion of a very large number of classic tinplate toys in a book primarily intended for the novice collector of limited means was that the prices of these items have now generally risen to a level that puts them beyond the reach of the average collector. Depending on condition, an early tinplate lorry or fire engine by a wellknown maker may now be expected to fetch anything between

£1,000 ($1,200) and £10,000 ($12,000) at auction. The latter figure was approached on more than one occasion in 1984-85 when fine tinplate vehicles by such makers as Bing and Märklin came under the hammer—while in the case of the finer toy boats by such makers, the upper figure in our range is that closest to the norm.

Even tinplate toys in well-worn condition—in our system of classification (see *page 26*), those ranging from "good" to "play-worn"—now fetch very considerable prices. We have referred to the work of Japanese and Far Eastern makers as "increasingly collectable": the truth of this assertion is borne out by the fact that even these toys are now going beyond the resources of many collectors, with good examples of such toys now approaching or exceeding three-figure sums.

As a result of the escalating prices of tinplate toys, most new collectors are turning their attention to diecast models, and in particular to the diecast models of more recent years. Therefore, a large part of this book is given over to diecast transport toys, with pride of place going, inevitably, to the models produced from the 1930s until *c*1980 by Dinky Toys of Great Britain and France, since these are by far the most popular diecast toys with collectors all over the world. Corgi and Lesney ("Models of Yesteryear") of Great Britain are well represented, and examples are shown also of the work of such makers as Britains of Great Britain, CIJ and Norev of France, Schuco of West Germany, Urango and Polistil of Italy, and Tootsietoy of the United States of America. As with tinplate toys, we have tried to avoid unnecessary duplication of models that were shown in "Metal Toys".

PEDAL-POWERED TOYS

No book on transport toys would be complete without coverage of pedal-powered vehicles, although the collector of these fascinating items will have to contend both with high prices (for restoration, since they are most ofen found in hard-worn condition, as well as initial purchase) and the problems of storage and display of models up to 6ft

(2m) long or more. But pedal vehicles were too attractive to be omitted, especially because, as in the case of "Metal Toys" and "Toy Cars", we were given access to the fine collection assembled by Shaun Magee at Bishop's Waltham, Hampshire. Pedal-powered transport toys are, of course, rarer than pedal cars, but we were able to assemble a number of unusual models that are shown on *pages 124-125*.

Our coverage is completed by one spread showing manufacturers' cata-logues (*pages 30-31*) and one spread illustrating packaging (*pages 32-33*). Maker's catalogues, which are now increasingly hard to find, are both attractive in their own right and also as an invaluable aid to in-depth research on models. And although some collectors and dealers may feel that "the box" has become something of a fetish and has made yet another contribution to the rising cost of collectable toys, it remains true that possession of the original box or packaging will, in most cases, add significantly to the market value of any model.

BEGINNING TO COLLECT

In spite of our somewhat grim remarks on rising prices, we hope to show the reader that it is neither difficult nor, necessarily, expensive to build up a satisfactory collection of transport toys—especially if some thought is given to the hobby before embarking on a series of purchases.

If you are new to the collecting

Above: *Fire Engine with Crank (a rear-mounted handle provides friction-drive for the rear wheels and revolves the hose drum) by "K", Japan; a fairly typical example of the brightly-printed tinplate toys issued by Japanese makers in the 1950s-60s. Length: 7·375in (18·7cm).*

modern tinplate items. Note, too, that while all tinplate toys are now increasing in value, some categories—in particular toy boats, and to a lesser extent aeroplanes; both of which are dealt with in separate sections below—are likely to prove even more expensive, because in they are in shorter supply, than the general run of tinplate toys. You are, we believe, most likely to decide on the collection of diecast models. (The collection of plastic models, whether ready-assembled or built from kits, is outside the scope of this book; however, a few part-plastic, part-metal toys will be found on the photographic spreads.)

The advantages of collecting diecast vehicles are many. They are fairly easily available: since the high cost of mould-making for individual models had to be recouped, they were usually produced in large numbers. They are durable, and are thus more likely to be found in good structural condition than the more vulnerable tinplate toys. They are generally smaller than tinplate toys, and are therefore much easier to store or display. They are cheaper and simpler to restore, if in very rough condition, than tinplate toys.

And, of course, diecast vehicles are cheaper to acquire than tinplate models. With certain exceptions, the most sought-after diecast vehicles, those made by Dinky Toys between 1934 and 1940, currently fetch prices of between £25 ($30) and £300 ($360), with even the scarcer items tending towards the middle of this range, while post-War

Dinky Toys fetch prices ranging from around £20-£30 ($25-$35) for models dating from the late 1940s to as little as £3 ($4) and upwards for models dating from the 1960s-70s. There are exceptions: a Leyland Octopus Wagon, (Dinky Supertoys Number 934, available from 1956 until 1954; see (7), *pages 68-69*) in near-mint condition and in a most unusual colour variation fetched a price of £820 ($984) at auction in 1985; we believe this to be a record price for a post-War diecast vehicle.

Finally, unlike tinplate toys, diecast models remain in large-scale production, and many attractive and collectable diecast vehicles are currently in production and are available at prices ranging from about 75p (90c) to £15 ($18) for large and detailed models in toyshops and model shops.

CHOOSING A THEME

Almost every type of vehicle, boat or aeroplane that has seen service in real life over the last eighty or so years is represented by a diecast model. The range of potential collectables is immense, and if the novice collector is wise, he will choose a theme before ever he buys a toy.

Although the exigencies of assembling material for photography have not always allowed us to be as consistent as we would have wished, we have attempted a broadly thematic presentation of the transport toys shown in this book. We have shown tinplate toys and diecast toys in separate sections, and within each section we have attempted to group them in types: lorries and vans; buses and trams; fire service vehicles; police cars; ambulances; agricultural vehicles; construction vehicles; boats; aeroplanes; pedal-powered vehicles. But even these thematic divisions, although

hobby, you must begin by deciding just what kind of material you hope to collect—and although our remarks in this essay are directed to the collector of transport toys, much of what we have to say is applicable to the collection of toys of all kinds.

You must first decide how much money you can devote to your hobby. Obviously, unless your financial resources are near-limitless, you will not decide on the collection of classic tinplate toys, or possibly even of more

suitable for visual presentation, are too wide-ranging to serve as a guide to themes for the individual collector, who will need to select a much narrower field of specialisation.

MUSEUMS AND TOYSHOPS

A visit to a museum may be productive of initial ideas for a theme. Most major museums in Europe and the United States now have on display toys of the past century, and there is a growing number of museums devoted exclusively to toys both ancient and modern. In Great Britain, a major collection of tinplate and diecast vehicles is on permanent display at the London Toy and Model Museum, while other fine specimens (with the emphasis on classic tinplate models) are to be found in the Bethnal Green Museum of Childhood, London, and the Museum of Childhood, Edinburgh.

Large toyshops will generally have on display a wide range of currently-available diecast vehicles (with some Far-Eastern-made tinplate toys), while more specialised model shops often have for sale a number of older models, both mint and second-hand. In the latter case, the novice collector will be able to obtain some idea of the kind of prices commanded by models that are no longer generally available.

AREAS OF SPECIALISATION

Following your initial research, you may be ready to decide upon a theme. Perhaps you will specialise in one type

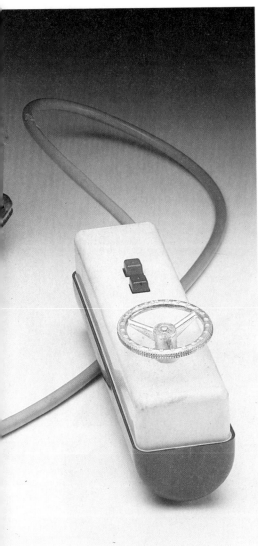

of vehicle: lorry, van, bus, taxi, fire engine, tractor, etc; perhaps in toy boats (in which case the emphasis, unless your pocket is bottomless, will be on diecast boats) or aeroplanes (again, most likely diecast aeroplanes of the kind shown on *pages 118-123*); perhaps in vehicles that carry advertising slogans (like the "Models of Yesteryear" vans shown on *pages 82-85*); or possibly in vehicles of all kinds by one particular maker.

If you have decided to specialise in one particular type of vehicle, it is as well to remember that there are literally hundreds of models of each type—such vehicles as fire engines, taxis, buses and lorries of all kinds have been perennially popular with toymakers and their customers—so you should try to fix on a single period and/or nationality. And if you have decided to collect the products of an individual maker, then remember that Dinky Toys, for example, issued more than 1,000 models (not counting colour and casting variations), many of them transport toys, and that other major makers, especially Corgi and Lesney, are hardly less prolific.

Suppose then, that your taste is for buses. Narrow this down to double-deck buses of a single period, say the 1960s. Find one of the increasing number of reference books now available, preferably one with an extensive check-list of models (a number of useful publications of this kind are listed at the end of this introduction) and find out which

makers produced models of the kind you desire. You will find that you can collect models made by Dinky Toys, Corgi Toys and Lesney ("Matchbox"), all of whom produced a fair number of models of British-built buses of the 1960s. You will also find that a few models that will fit into your collection were made by Lone Star (Impy) of Great Britain and some other minor makers.

Our example, of course, is just one possible field of specialisation. Your choice might equally well be for fire engines of the post-War period, vans with advertising of the 1960s, heavy plant, articulated trucks, or agricultural vehicles—but in all cases, a check on just what material is available in the category is necessary before you begin to purchase models. Make sure that the possibility of an attractive and well-balanced collection exists—and that the assembly of such a collection is possible with the financial resources available to you.

COLLECTING TOY BOATS

Produced in types ranging from rowing boats to liners (warships, of course, are outside the scope of this book), and in sizes ranging from a few inches to more than three feet (1m) long, toy boats are among the most beautiful and desirable of all toys, as the selection illustrated on *pages 108-113* will show. Sadly, however, we must repeat the warning that we have already given: they are among the most scarce and costly of all toys and

few people will be able to afford to build up a good collection.

Not only are many toy boats comparatively fragile in terms of rigging and other details, the "water-borne" examples are also particularly subject to accidental loss. One collector suggested to us that a profitable "salvage company" might be formed to raise the many sunken wrecks of classic tinplate boats that now lie on the bottoms of lakes and ponds in public parks all over the world!

Since tinplate boats that were intended to operate in water were normally hand-soldered and hand-painted, to ensure their waterproof durability, they were generally highly-priced in comparison with toys of other kinds, and although production runs might be long-lasting, they were often not produced in large numbers. Thus, a toy boat by a wellknown maker, in good condition, will command a high price on the modern collector's market: four-figure sums are relatively common, and a fine tinplate boat by a maker like Märklin might be expected to

Above: *A mouth-watering display of boxed diecast model ships by Dinky Toys. (Left) Le Transatlantique "La Normandie", made by Dinky Toys, France, but marketed as No 52c in Great Britain, 1935-39. (Centre) "Famous Liners", Set No 51, by Dinky Toys, Great Britain, 1935-40: "Europa", "Rex", "Empress of Britain", "Strathaird", "Queen of Bermuda" and "Britannic". (Right) "Queen Mary", No 52a, available boxed, with rollers, 1935-40, and unboxed in 1947-49. All are now limited or scarce.*

Left: *SR.N6 Hovercraft by Dinky Toys, Great Britain; Dinky Toys No 290, issued in 1970 and available until 1976. The same casting was used for the Military Hovercraft, No 281, 1973-75, which had a gun in place of the radar scanner. The hovercraft has an opening front hatch; the scanner and propeller revolve as it is pushed along. Length: 5·47in (139mm).*

proach five figures in the auction room.

American makers were among the earliest to produce metal mechanical boats: the firm of Ives, Blakeslee and Company, Bridgeport, Connecticut, was producing clockwork rowing boats by about 1875, and even before that date such firms as Stevens and Brown, Cromwell, Connecticut, were producing "carpet toy" push/pull-along boats, often in cast iron, a material much favoured in both the 19th and 20th centuries by American toymakers.

EARLY MAKERS

In Europe, the most famous early makers of metal toy boats were Radiguet (Radiguet et Massiot after 1889) of France and Jean Schoenner of Nuremburg, Germany. It is now rare to find a Radiguet boat in good condition, and rarer still to encounter an early example by Schoenner, a maker active only from c1875 until c1906 and one whose boats usually bear no trademark. Although production was not large until the first decade of the 20th century, the great German tradition of high-quality metal boats was established from the 1890s, when such makers as Bing, Carette, Märklin and Plank entered the field, and were soon followed in production by Fleischmann, Hess and Lehmann.

Many collectors would say (and on the evidence of present-day auction prices many more would agree) that of all the famous German makers, Märklin is the finest. The firm's output of the pre-World War I period, especially, includes many of the most splendid examples of the genre. The earlier models are largely hand-painted and have such details as port-holes hand-painted also, although applied transfers and rubber-stamping for details came into use quite soon: the "Luzern" liner by Märklin shown at (1), *pages 110-111*, dating from after World War I, although in a style differing little from earlier examples, has rubber-stamped port-holes. Fabric flags are fitted to earlier Märklin boats—the firm did not fit tinplate flags, usually hand-painted, until after World War I—and like other makers Märklin would fit the same model with different flags and furnish it with an appropriate name for sale in various foreign markets.

The collector is more likely to encounter good-quality boats by other German makers, notably Gebrüder Bing, a firm perhaps second in importance in this field only to Märklin and one whose pre-World War I boats are to be found in much greater number. Bing's very wide range extended from liners (as well as warships) to motorboats and to small "novelty" waterborne toys. A most interesting steamboat by Bing, dating from around 1906, fitted with a small steam-turbine engine, and incorporating in its construction items from Bing's toy railway range, is shown at (6), *pages 108-109*.

CARETTE AND OTHER MAKERS

Georges Carette, a French national working in Nuremburg until World War I (his company was, for some reason, called George Carette & Cie), produced both large boats of fine quality, which are now rarely encountered—like the fine River Boat of *c*1906 (1) and the Paddle Steamer of *c*1911 (3), *pages 108-109*—and small, low-priced toys. Many of Carette's boats bear no trademarks, and attribution depends upon information from contemporary catalogues and on the characteristic style of such details as ships' boats. The hulls of Carette's boats are sometimes of zinc rather than tinplate, and the same hull-shapes appear in boats by Fleischmann—for example, see the set of Liners at (7-10), *pages 110-111*—since that firm acquired much of Carette's tooling after 1917. Fleischmann's boats of the 1930s reached a high standard and a number of the firm's models, notably a liner made in no less than eleven hull lengths, from 6·6in (16cm) to 31·5in (80cm), appeared in the same form both before and after World War II.

The firm of Hess, Nuremburg, in production until the 1930s, was noted for its clockwork-powered "carpet toy" boats, as was Lehmann, a Nuremburg firm better-known for its novelty toys. The Arnold Company also deserves special mention because it was, along with Fleischmann, about the last to maintain the German tradition of tinplate boats after World War II—see particularly the liners shown at (3-6), *pages 110-111*—until the increasing use of plastic construction, along with the aggressive marketing of Japanese tinplate toys, rendered uneconomical the production of comparatively expensive tinplate boats by Western makers.

CONDITION OF BOATS

Since toys boats generally saw fairly tough and hazardous service, examples in good condition, especially from the earlier years, are more rarely encountered than is the case with most other transport toys. Such details as ships' boats, anchors, flags, and especially rigging, are frequently missing—and if present, they may prove to be replacement items. Many boats will have been repaired or even completely restored. However, if the restoration has been

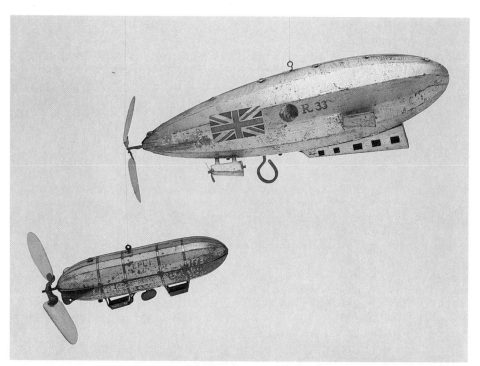

expertly carried out (as is the case with the restored examples noted among the boats shown in this book) it will not detract from the boat's appeal or significantly affect its value.

As with other toys, possession of the original packaging is desirable. Here, however, it should be noted that the earlier models of the highest quality were often marketed in robust but fairly plain boxes of wood or heavy cardboard: it was on the cheaper toys that colourfully-printed pictorial labels more often featured.

Unless the collector has great and

well-founded faith in his own ability, the restoration or mechanical repair of toy boats is best entrusted to the hands of a professional. Ideally, boats should be displayed on purpose-made stands or some similar securing device, in glazed cabinets, at an even temperature, away from damp and out of direct sunlight, which may fade colours.

TOY AEROPLANES

Although toy aeroplanes did not, of course, attract the attention of toy-makers until some time after the Wright Brothers' first flights at Kitty Hawk,

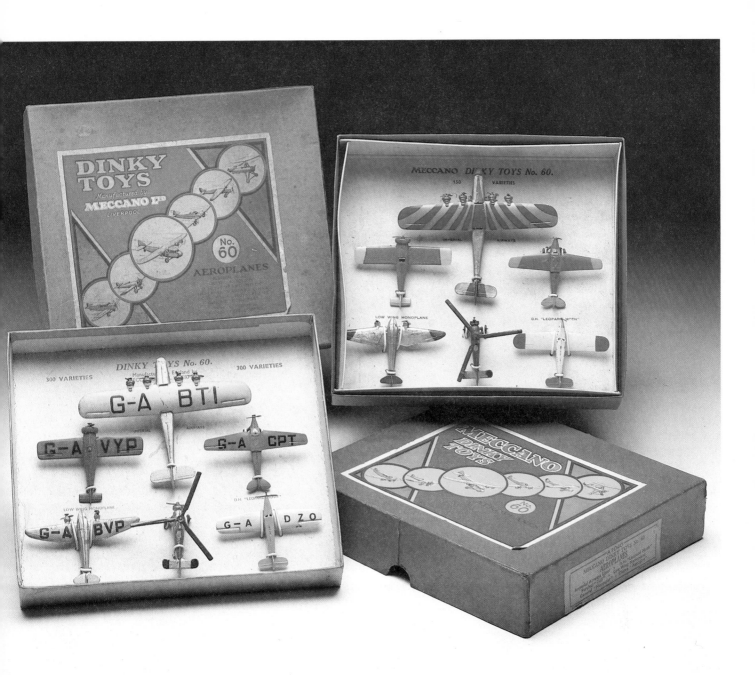

Top left: *The clockwork "EPL I" Zeppelin (lower left) by Lehmann, Germany, was among the earlier aeronautical toys, appearing from c1910 into the 1920s. It is 7·5in (19cm) long. The "R.33" airship is of a somewhat later date.*

Left: *A boxed set of aeroplanes by Dinky Toys, France; issued as No 60 in 1957, renumbered 501 in 1959 and available until 1962. It contains (top to bottom): S-58 Sikorsky Helicopter; Mystère IV A (G.A.M.D.) (left) and Vauture Sud Aviation (right); Lockheed Super Constellation G.*

Above: *A boxed set of aeroplanes by Dinky Toys, Great Britain; Dinky Toys No 60, issued in June 1934 and available until 1940. The set is shown in two finishes: (right) as originally issued; (left) as it appeared in 1936-39. It was briefly available in camouflage finish in 1940. It comprises (left to right; top to bottom): Imperial Airways Liner (No 60a); Low Wing Monoplane (No 60d); DH "Leopard Moth" (No 60b); General "Monospar" (No 60e); Cierva Autogiro (No 60f); Percival "Gull" (No 60c). This boxed set is now very scarce in any finish.*

North Carolina, in 1903, aeronautical toys based on balloons and dirigibles was made as early as the 1890s. These tinplate toys, now very scarce, were mostly of the "novelty" type: a fairly typical example consisted of a "hot-air balloon" of hollow tinplate, its envelope concealing a clockwork mechanism that powered the antics of the figure of an acrobat slung beneath it.

Rather more common in this early period, although scarce and expensive today, were tinplate representations of Zeppelin-type airships—like those shown on *page 14* (top left)—which were produced by such famous German makers as Lehmann and Märklin from c1908 onwards. Most toy Zeppelins, and early tinplate aircraft in general, had clockwork motors of sufficient power to enable them to "fly" in a circle, with the help of somewhat over-sized propellers, when suspended from the ceiling by a cord.

EARLY TINPLATE PLANES

German makers led the field in the production of mechanical tinplate toys of all kinds before World War I, and it was not until the powers of the Wright biplane has been triumphantly displayed in Europe in 1908 that aeroplanes began to figure significantly in the catalogues of such makers as Bing, Günthermann, Märklin and Plant. By 1909, Märklin's catalogue listed a tinplate Wright biplane in three sizes, the largest with a wingspan of 17·3in (44cm), with a clockwork motor that enabled it to taxi on rubber-tyred wheels or, driving a large celluloid pusher-propeller, to "fly" along a wire. In the same year Günthermann produced a toy inspired by the cross-Channel aviator Louis Bleriot and involving an alternative method of "flight": the clockwork-powered monoplane was mounted at one end of a counter-weighted rod that was pivoted on a central metal pillar.

All these early aeronautical toys, even including small "penny toy" aeroplanes, are now scarce and valuable. The average collector is more likely to encounter the tinplate aeroplanes produced after World War I, when the wartime demonstrations of air power had considerably stimulated the interest of toymakers and their customers—although aeroplanes, it should be noted, were never at any time as popular with the toy-buying public as wheeled vehicles or boats. Nevertheless, from about the mid-1920s, by which time the major German makers had recovered from the setbacks inflicted by World War I, the rapid expansion of commercial aviation and the great excitement caused by various "record flights"—see (16), *pages 118-119*, for a diecast model by Dinky Toys inspired by one of the record-breakers—led to the issue of an increasing number of tinplate aeroplanes.

Among the wellknown makers producing tinplate aeronautical toys in the 1920s-30s, the names of Distler, Fleischmann, Günthermann and Tipp of Germany, Jep and Joustra of

Right: *A selection of diecast aeroplanes made before World War II by Dinky Toys, Great Britain. Shown with their boxes are (bottom left) The King's Aeroplane (Airspeed Envoy) (No 62k; 1938-41); (left) "Explorer" (Armstrong Whitworth) Airliner (No 62p; 1938-41, 1945-49); (left to right thereafter) "Singapore" Flying Boat (No 60h; 1936-41), shown in two different colour finishes with variations in registration lettering; Percival "Gull" (No 60k; 1938-41), as issued in a souvenir box to commemorate H.L. Brook's record South African flight; (top right) "Ensign" (Armstrong Whitworth) Airliner (No 62p; 1938-41, 1945-49), another of the several finishes in which this model appeared. In the foreground is the instruction sheet, packaged in the boxes of some pre-War models, for "Gliding" the toys: the eyed hook fitted to earlier models for this purpose is clearly to be seen on the red-finished "Singapore" Flying Boat.*

Below: *The dire effects of "metal fatigue" are clearly seen in this view of Dinky Toys No 67a, Junkers Ju 89 (1940-41).*

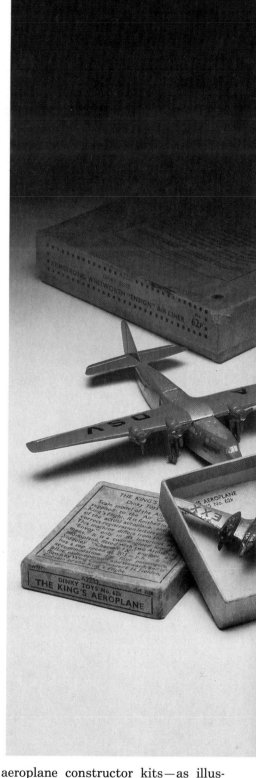

France, and Cardini of Italy are prominent. Aeroplanes by Joustra (7), Güunthermann (8), and a British maker of this period (6), are shown on *pages 112-113*. Toy warplanes became increasingly popular, for grimly obvious reasons, in the 1930s, and at the same time the earlier "space toys" began to appear in the shape of tinplate rocket-ships.

After World War II, "space toys" tended to flourish at the expense of conventional aeroplanes, although both German and, especially, Japanese makers continued to produce aeroplanes of quite high quality in tinplate (although often with plastic details) of

the kind shown on *pages 114-115*. Also worthy of note are the tinplate helicopters shown on *pages 116-117*: in the ingenious toys produced by Arnold, West Germany, the "novelty" tradition of the earliest aeronautical toys, as noted above, is revealed as being far from extinct. The more recent tinplate aeroplanes by Far Eastern and a few Western makers are likely to become increasingly collectable as the aircraft that they depict pass further from service and from everyday memory.

CONSTRUCTOR KITS

From 1931 onward, Meccano of Great Britain introduced a series of

aeroplane constructor kits—as illustrated in the Meccano catalogue for 1938-39, shown at (9), *pages 30-31*—featuring the nut-and-bolt assembly of metal parts. Very late in the decade, these kits were available with parts in camouflage finish or in grey, as well as in the usual blue-and-white. From the larger kits, which included the diecast half-figure of a pilot, a number of different types of aeroplanes could be built, and a clockwork motor specially adapted to power wheels and propellers could be purchased.

Constructor kits incorporating a greater number of diecast parts, giving a more realistic overall appearance,

along with composition figures of aircrew, were made in Germany at the same period by Märklin, but most of these depicted military aircraft.

DIECAST AEROPLANES

Until fairly recently, diecast aeroplanes were generally considered to be of less interest to collectors than diecast vehicles. However, they are now becoming increasingly collectable and, as with vehicles, the attention of most collectors is likely to centre on the extensive range made by Dinky Toys of Great Britain and France from the 1930s onward. A good collection of these models is shown on *pages 118-123*,

along with examples of a number of the "Nicky Toys" made in India from obsolete Dinky Toys dies, and models by such makers as Schuco of West Germany, CIJ of France, Mercury of Italy, and Corgi Toys of Great Britain.

The earliest Dinky Toys issued were mainly of civil aeroplanes and, as was also the case with tinplate toys, flying boats were especially popular: from our extensive selection of these, note particularly the Mayo Composite Aircraft at (3), *pages 120-121*, now scarce. Some of the earlier Dinky Toys biplanes will also now be hard to find. As war approached, the number of military aircraft issued increased, and

by the later 1930s models were available in camouflage finish as well as in the silver (aluminium) finish shown in our illustrations, which was used both pre- and post-War. It is worth noting, also, that some Dinky Toys aeroplanes, like the wheeled vehicles of the period, were issued in boxed sets, as shown above.

WEAK POINTS

In some diecast aeroplanes of the 1930s, tinplate was used for wings, but metal fatigue, manifested as "wing droop", is all too common on Dinky Toys diecast models. Propellers, too, are a vulnerable point, but replacements

are available if these should be found to be missing. In the case of post-World War II issues, possession of the original box is particularly important for value—and in any case, diecast aeroplanes are best stored in their boxes, at an even temperature.

A number of the post-War Dinky Toys aeroplanes are, like most pre-War issues, now in short supply, for from the later 1950s onward the increasing popularity of constructor kits in plastic, made by such firms as Airfix, severely limited the sales, and consequently the production runs, of diecast models of several kinds.

ACQUIRING TOYS

We have given, above, brief histories of the development of toys boats and toy aeroplanes, the more exotic of the transport toys shown in this book. We will not, however, attempt to do the same for the much larger category of wheeled vehicles, since this would involve much repetition and, in the limited space available, leave the reader little the wiser. The reader's attention is directed to the Introduction to our companion volume, "Toy Cars", and to Salamander's "Metal Toys",

where much general information on the history of tinplate and diecast transport toys will be found, as well as to the relevant titles listed at the end of this Introduction. Here, we believe, it will be of greater help to the reader to provide a guide to the acquisition of items for a collection of transport toys.

WHERE TO BUY TOYS

As we have already noted, some very collectable transport toys are currently available in toy and model shops, and these will present few problems other than that of sticking to your budget. The location of older, scarcer models will require rather more effort.

Watch the "For Sale" advertisements in your local newspapers (the "free" newspapers distributed in most areas usually carry a wealth of such small-ads), and remember that other collectors will be watching them too, so you will need to move fast if a bargain seems to be on offer! Watch out also for notices of house clearance sales, usually organised by local estate agents: tinplate and early diecast models may sometimes be acquired as part of mixed lots of "toys", along with a fair amount of junk.

Above: *Fire Services Gift Set by Dinky Toys, Great Britain; No 957, issued in 1959 and in production until 1964. Now hard to find, this boxed set consists of a Fire Chief's Car (Canadian Type), No 257, based on the Nash Rambler casting, in production 1961-68 and shown here in front of the box; Turntable Fire Escape (above in box), No 956, 1958-71; Fire Engine, No 555 (later 955), 1952-69.*

Above right: *Election Mini-Van, No 492, by Dinky Toys, Great Britain. Issued in October 1964 and available only until 1965, this model is now fairly scarce. Bearing the slogan "Vote for Somebody", it has opening doors and a plastic loudspeaker and was marketed, as shown, complete with the plastic figure of a parliamentary candidate with microphone and cable. Length: 3·071in (78mm).*

If you are an optimist, you will frequent jumble sales, although the toys to be found there have usually cross the "play-worn" barrier to reach the "scrap-metal" category! Try putting your own advertisements in the local press, but be prepared to deal with vendors offering battered, wheel-less wrecks at ridiculous prices: everyone now knows that "old toys" may be valuable; unfortunately, many non-collectors seem to equate poor condition with antiquity and desirability.

Although you are not so likely to locate amazing bargains, the specialist press may be rewarding. Hobby magazines tend to come and go, so watch your local newsagent's counter. Make a point of buying "Exchange and Mart" (which has a special "Toys" section) in Britain, or "Antique Toy World" in the United States. A subscription to the magazine "Modellers' World" will also be well worthwhile. Specialist magazines for car buffs also often carry features and advertising relating to models of cars and transport toys—and in these specialist publications you will also find advance notices of "auto-jumbles" and "swap-meets".

AUTO-JUMBLES AND SWAP-MEETS

An auto-jumble, as its name suggests, is a bring-and-buy sale organised by and for transport enthusiasts: at the major venues it is a rule that *all* articles for sale must be transport-related. There will usually be a few model dealers in attendance, and the "jumble" stalls themselves are quite likely to have

Below: *Post vehicles and accessories by Dinky Toys. (Clockwise) Telephone Service Van, No 261 (Britain), 1956-61; Royal Mail Van ("EIIR" decal), No 260 (Britain), 1955-61; Royal Mail Van ("GR"), No 34b (Britain), 1938-40 and 1946-52; colour variant of No 34b; "Postes" Van, No 25C (France), 1954-57; "Postes" Van, No 25BV (France), 1954-59; Post Office Van (Citroën), No 560 (France), 1963-70; Renault 4 PTT Van, No 561 (France), 1968-72. The Postmen, Pillar Boxes and Telephone Boxes are by Dinky Toys, Great Britain.*

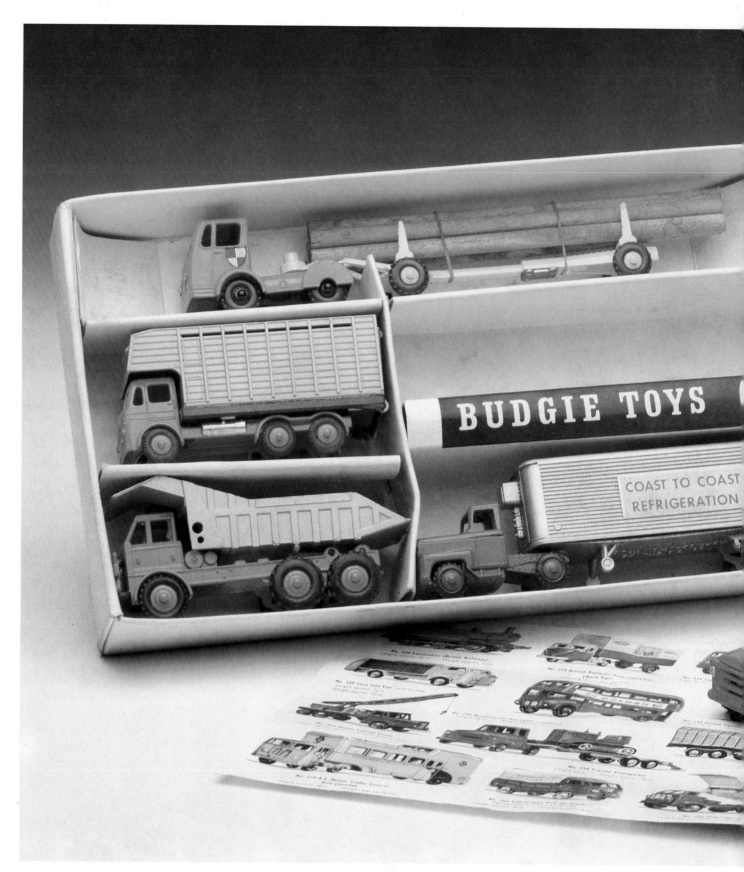

models for sale. Be warned, however, that at venues where non-professional dealers are in the majority there is a chance that the prices asked will be higher than those that would be expected from a specialist dealer or a knowledgeable collector. Non-professional vendors, sometimes influenced by an imperfect understanding of "price guides", will often considerably over-value their stock.

More expert value-judgements are likely to be encountered at swap-meets, which are organised by members of the collecting fraternity in order to buy, sell or exchange toys among themselves. You may not find bargains—although it is surprising how often one collector's "rubbish" proves to be just what the other collector was looking for—but you will learn a great deal from just looking and listening. And if you do buy, prices will be fair—but always examine any potential purchase very carefully, and never be afraid to bargain with the vendor.

BUYING FROM DEALERS

It is becoming increasingly common for model shops to run a second-hand dealership along with the marketing of current models, and there are, of course, many dealers who specialise in old toys either exclusively or as part of a general antiques business. Dealers are in business to make money and, since they usually have to cover considerable overheads beyond the cost of their stock, their prices cannot be low.

A dealer's "mark-up", that is, the

Although its models were of good quality, Budgie Toys was unable to survive in the British market dominated in the 1950s-60s by Dinky, Corgi and Lesney. Gift Set No 5 consists of a Timber Transporter (No 230), Cattle Truck (No 220), Foden Dump Truck (N0 226), Refrigerator Articulated Truck (No 202) and Tractor Transporter (No 234).

price he asks for an article above what he himself paid for it, may be anything from around 20 per cent on a fairly expensive toy that he feels may be difficult to sell, to 100 per cent or more on a cheaper item which he knows is very much in demand. However, a dealer without regular customers will not stay in business for long, so sharp practice, which may work once but is guaranteed to drive away customers in the long run, and rank profiteering, are much rarer than is sometimes supposed.

Do your best to find an expert, trustworthy dealer—ideally through recommendations by fellow-collectors —and try to establish a good relationship with him. An initial purchase, not necessarily of an expensive item, should give you a chance to ask for advice on any similar models that may be available. If you seem likely to become a regular customer, plenty of good advice will be forthcoming; and once you are recognised as a serious collector, even if not a big spender

(speaking from personal experience, we can say that most dealers value a modestly-spending regular customer more highly than the occasional pluto-crat), it may well be that interesting items will be reserved for your first refusal and that part-exchanges for your unwanted or duplicated models may be arranged.

Having begun your collection with models purchased from dealers, from fellow-collectors, at swap-meets and from similar sources, you will probably

Above: *Three large diecast vehicles in the "Major Models" series produced by Lincoln International, Hong Kong, in the 1950s-60s. The Timber Truck, shown on its box, has a load that consists of a wooden block that is scored to resemble a pile of planks, secured by gilt metal chains. The Front End Loader has a working bucket and an operating steering wheel. The Dump Truck has a spring-loaded tipping body, operated by a lever to the left of the cab, and an opening tailboard. Length (each model): 8·25in (21cm).*

Top left: *A line-up of Jeeps demonstrates the popularity of this vehicle with both makers and collectors. (Left, top to bottom): Hotchkiss Willys Jeep, No 80B, Dinky Toys, France, 1958-59; Jeep, No 25y (later 405), Dinky Toys, Great Britain, 1952-64; Jeep, Nicky Toys, India; Willys Jeep, No 1322, Solido, France. (Right, top to bottom): Jeep, No 25j, Dinky Toys, Great Britain, 1947-48; colour variant of No 25j; colour variant of No 25j; colour and wheel variant of No 80B.*

Left: *Bedford Long Wheelbase Tipper, No 276; another of the good-quality but short-lived diecast models produced by Budgie Toys, Great Britain, and now of limited availability. Length: 5in (127mm).*

sooner or later think of buying or selling at auction. The major international auction houses, such as Sotheby's, Christies and Phillips, now regularly hold special toy sales in which model vehicles feature prominently.

AUCTION HOUSES

The collector must not assume that because an auction house has a famous name it is only interested in dealing with very valuable items. Early in 1985, within a few weeks of the house's much-publicised handling of a painting that attracted bids of up to £8 million, Sotheby's held a toy sale in which the prices fetched by lots containing diecast vehicles ranged from £18 ($22) to around £300 ($360).

If you are nervous about venturing on to the auction circuit, remember that the auction houses are always willing to give advice on their buying and selling procedures. And even if you never make a purchase or sell a toy, attending as many auctions as possible

will help you to attain a good knowledge of the current values attached to toys of all kinds.

For most auctions of any size, an advance catalogue will be available at least a fortnight beforehand. This will contain detailed descriptions of all the toys on offer, together with the auction house's estimates of the prices the various lots are expected to fetch (for the benefit of those wishing to make postal bids). Obviously, it will be well worth buying the catalogue, which will cost you no more than the price of a current diecast model, whether or not you intend to go to the sale.

HANDLING RARE TOYS

If you are thinking of bidding at an auction, you must be sure to attend the "views": the times appointed before the sale when the forthcoming lots may be examined by potential purchasers. Even if you do not intend to buy, the view may give you the opportunity to see and handle rare toys.

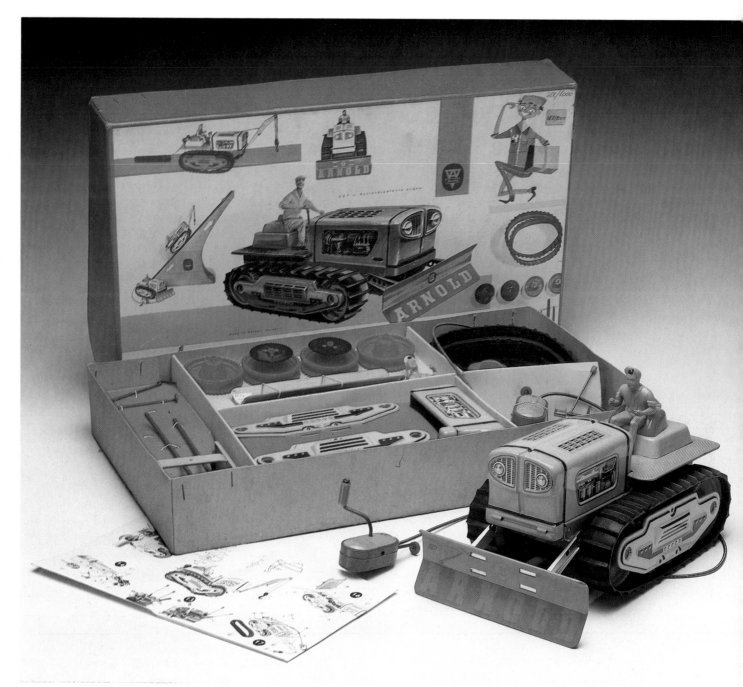

If you are buying, remember that items are bought at auction not only "as seen", but also "as catalogued". Thus, if you buy a toy that proves to be not as described in the catalogue, you may ask to have your money refunded. Remember, too, when it comes to paying for your purchase, that many auction houses now levy a "buyer's premium" of some 10 per cent, to which Value Added Tax (VAT) must be added (in the United Kingdom).

SELLING TOYS AT AUCTION

Rare or unusual toys are probably better sold at auction than elsewhere, since in the case of the more speculative items this may be the only way of establishing their true value on the open market. In the case of transport toys, this will apply particularly to items of the classic tinplate period by lesser-known makers. For the vendor of diecast vehicles, the only problem will be that of making up a satisfactory "lot".

Most major auction houses will accept for sale lots, ie, either single toys or collections, which they estimate to have a minimum value of around £50 ($60). (If you are buying at auction, this may mean that you will have to purchase some toys that you do not want in order to acquire one or two items that you really need—but, of course, these surplus models can form part of your stock to be disposed of at the next swap-meet.)

A reserve price (that is, a price below which the lot shall not be sold) is agreed between the vendor and the auctioneer, and the lot is then ready to be catalogued and put up for sale. The reserve price must be realistic, for if the lot does not reach its reserve and is unsold, a "not sold commission" may be payable by the vendor. You should note, also, that a successful sale will entail payment to the auction house by the vendor of a commission of around 10-15 per cent. (The conditions described

in the foregoing paragraph will, of course, vary somewhat from one auction house to another.)

THE VALUE OF MODELS

What is an individual model worth? The answer is the product of an equation involving four major factors. These are, not necessarily in order of importance: condition; rarity; desirability; availability. Every collector must work out this equation in terms of his own speciality. However, as we have said, you will be able to get a good idea of current values by regular attendance at auctions, and you can also send for the lists of models offered for sale by various dealers in the columns of the specialist journals.

With the ever-increasing interest in toy collecting, many reference books, some of them highly specialised and dealing with the output of one toymaker only, have been forthcoming from publishers all over the world. Side by

Above left: *Remote-control Bulldozer by Arnold, West Germany, dating from the later 1950s. This high-quality toy was marketed both ready-assembled and as a construction kit, shown here with its instruction leaflet. The major parts are tinplate with printed details; the drive wheels are plastic, with wooden idler wheels for the black rubber tracks; and the driver is plastic. The toy is powered by a mechanism utilising a cored cable from a hand-cranked control set, with a plunger that steers the vehicle. Length overall: 11·375in (28·89cm).*

Top centre: *"Swallow" Scooter; a cheap and cheerful toy of pressed and printed tinplate (note that the driver's coat and arms are separate pressings) by an unidentified Japanese maker of the 1950s. This friction-powered toy runs on three rubber wheels. Length: 3·75in (95mm).*

Top right: *The large diecast Motor Scooter is by Tekno, Denmark, and dates from the 1950s. The Civilian Motorcyclist, shown in two colour variants, is by Dinky Toys, Great Britain; No 37a, available from 1937-40, and also from 1947-55.*

Above: *These diecast motorcycle models, Racing Sidecar Outfit, No 264, and A.A. Motor Cycle Patrol, No 452, were made by Budgie Toys, the trade name of Morris & Stone (London) Ltd, in the later 1950s. The boxes have a black-and-yellow colour scheme strongly reminiscent of the packaging used by Dinky Toys, whose then dominant position in the British market contributed to Budgie's failure to survive. The brochure gives some idea of the maker's wide range, which included lorries, vans, buses, fire engines and police cars, as well as military models.*

side with these have come a number of more-or-less specific "price guides".

These can be most useful—and we ourselves are much indebted to the compilers of the "Swapmeet and Toy Fair Catalogue of British Die-Cast Model Toys" (listed along with other recommended titles on *page 29*) for some of the value judgements in this book—but a word of caution is necessary. The information in price guides must always be interpreted in terms of current market conditions.

It must always be remembered that the prices quoted usually refer to toys in at least "very good" condition, and that the prices are generally based on auction records. Prices at auction may vary widely in accordance with a number of imponderables: the venue, the presence or absence of major dealers and collectors, the "mood" of the bidding (it is not unknown for prices to go "over the top" because of excessive enthusiasm on the part of the bidders), and so on.

For three reasons, this book is not a price guide. First, it is intended for an international readership, and prices vary considerably from country to country. Secondly, price guides fairly quickly become outdated (the best are regularly up-dated), and it is hoped that this work of colour reference may be of use to collectors of transport toys for many years to come. Thirdly, this book is primarily intended as an introduction to the pleasure that can be derived from collecting transport toys, not as a guide to collecting them for their investment value.

We have, however, attempted in the captions for many of the models to give some indication of the subject's comparative rarity in comparison with other models of the same kind (eg, when we say that a Dinky Toy is rare, we mean that is rare in comparison with other Dinky Toys of the same type and period; and likewise for models by other makers).

A GUIDE TO CONDITION

The desirability of a model will, of course, depend on the taste of the individual collector. On rarity, we offer the guidelines outlined above. Availability the collector will judge from his experience of dealers, swap-meets and auctions. What of the fourth element of this value equation: condition?

Although the collector must always endeavour to acquire toys that are in the best possible condition, it is inevitable that there will be times when a much-desired specimen is only available in less than fine condition. This is especially the case with such items as pedal-powered vehicles, which were meant for active play and took hard knocks; toy boats, for the reasons described above; and such models as aeroplanes, helicopters, fire engines and cranes, with their vulnerable propellers, rotors, ladders, jibs etc. All tinplate toys are liable to corrosion, as well as loss of parts, while some earlier diecast toys are subject to metal fatigue.

As a guide to potential purchasers, auction houses and reputable dealers usually grade the toys they offer in terms similar to those that follow.

Mint:

As new, in its original box (if a boxed item) and with the box itself in good condition. If the box or packaging is not in fine original condition, the description "Factory Fresh" is sometimes applied, rather than "Mint".

Very Good:

The toy shows slight wear, possibly with some damage to or fading of its finish, but with all its parts complete and undamaged. It may or may not be in the original box or packaging.

Good:

A sound example of the toy, but with noticeable wear from handling and use, and lacking its original box or packaging.

Play-Worn:

As the term implies, this designates a toy which has seen considerable use: it may have damaged or missing parts and it may have been repainted. Unless it is a rare or much-desired model, the collector should consider carefully the price asked before deciding to buy a toy in this condition, and should ask himself whether it will be possible for him to re-sell it, if he can subsequently acquire a better example, at a later date.

Right: *The diecast 1922 AEC "General" S-Type Omnibus, "Models of Yesteryear" No Y-23 (First Issue), by Lesney, Great Britain, was issued in 1983 and remains available. Note the variations in the colours of the "Schweppes" logo: a version with the logo in red on white is much scarcer than the examples shown.*

Below right: *1920 Rolls Royce Fire Engine, "Borough Green & District", "Models of Yesteryear" No Y-6 (Fourth Issue), was first issued in 1977 and is currently available. The first version is shown here: the second version (1982) has red seats, and the third version (1983) has black seats and a white plastic ladder.*

Below: *Petrol Pumps, No 49, issued in 1935—note the brand names!—by Dinky Toys, Great Britain (to supplement the Garage, No 45, 1935-41); available until 1941 and again post-War until 1955.*

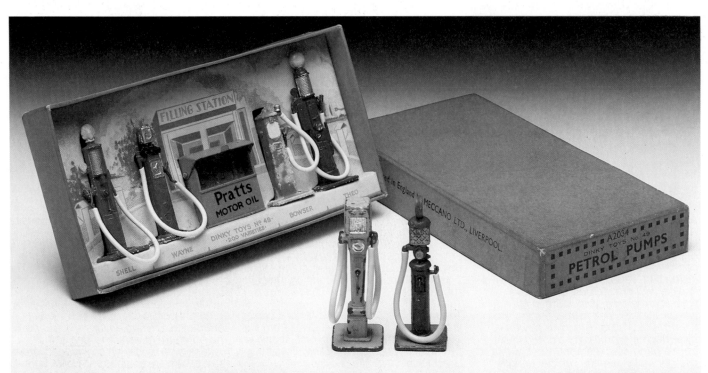

RESTORING TOYS

If you should decide to purchase a rare toy in "play-worn" condition, you may consider having it restored as nearly as possible to its original condition. This will, of course apply mainly to tinplate toys, since apart from the fitting of reproduction parts, which are available for Dinky Toys and some other leading makes, there is little to be done to restore diecast models. There are some collectors whose main interest lies in restoration and who will purchase tinplate toys in well-worn condition simply for this purpose.

However, the average collector is best advised to entrust the work of restoration to a professional. The process will not be cheap but,properly done, it will enhance both the appearance and the value of the toy; amateur restoration will generally add little to the appearance and will certainly detract from the value.

If you envisage selling the toy at some time in the future, it may be better to leave it unrestored, since many collectors will always prefer an unrestored item, however play-worn, to one far-removed from its original condition. As a rough guide, it may be said that in the case of a rare toy restoration—depending always on the amount and the quality of the work that has been done—may reduce the value of the toy by some 20-30 per cent. In the case of less-important models, restoration may more than halve the value.

DISPLAYING MODELS

How you choose to display your collection will, of course, depend very much on its size and on the amount of space at your disposal. Ideally, both tinplate and diecast toys should be displayed in glazed cabinets: on open shelves, they will gather dust and will become unpleasantly grubby in a surprisingly short time. Regular cleaning will be necessary, but this must always be kept to the absolute minimum.

Diecast models can be dusted or cleaned with a soft brush to remove dirt from their crevices. Greater care must be taken with tinplate models: if they become particularly discoloured by dirt, the tinplate may be cleaned with mild soap and warm water and a final polish given with good-quality car-wax and a soft, dry cloth. The mechanism of clockwork-powered models should be kept very slightly oiled. Whatever the method of display, the models should not be exposed to direct sunlight, which will cause paint finishes to fade. The models should also be kept at an even temperature, for wide variations in temperature may "wake up" the incompatible alloys used in some earlier diecast models, thus contributing to metal fatigue.

Above: *1927 Talbot Van, "Lipton's Tea", "Models of Yesteryear" No Y-5 (Fourth Issue), by Lesney, Great Britain. On the left is the first, scarcer type (1978) with Royal Crest; on the right, the revised version (1980), without Crest.*

Below: *Four versions of the 1918 Crossley Wagon, "Models of Yesteryear" No Y-13 (Third Issue). (Clockwise): R.A.F. Tender (1974)—the 1976 version with olive canopy is scarcer; "Carlsberg" Beer Wagon (1983); "Löwenbräu" Brewery Wagon (1984); "Evans Bros Coal & Coke" Wagon (1979).*

Right: *The 1912 Ford Model "T" Van, "Models of Yesteryear" No Y-12 (Third Issue), has appeared in more than a dozen versions in 1975-85. (Clockwise): "Smith's Potato Crisps", with blue-white-and-gold logo and silver trim; "Smith's Potato Crisps" (1981), with red-and-white logo and gold trim; two versions of "Harrods Express Delivery Motor Accessories" (1982), in gold and silver trim respectively. The first version of this model has rear doors with a double line; the second version has cast-in rear doors and black seats; the third version is equipped with tan seats.*

Tin Toys 1945-1975 (London, 1978)
Michael Buhler

Discovering Toys and Toy Museums (Aylesbury, 1971)
Pauline Flick

An Illustrated History of Toys (London, 1965)
Karl Fritzsch & Manfred Bachman

The Price Guide to Metal Toys (Suffolk, 1980)
The Price Guide and Identification of Automobilia (Suffolk, 1982)
The All-Colour Directory of Metal Toys (London, 1984)
Gordon Gardiner & Alistair Morris

The Collector's All-Colour Guide to Toy Cars (London, 1985)
Gordon Gardiner & Richard O'Neill

A History of British Dinky Toys 1934-1964 (Hemel Hempstead, 1966)
Commercial Vehicles (London, 1970)
Cecil Gibson

Catalogue of Model Cars of the World *(includes transport toys)*
(Lausanne, Switzerland, 1967)
Jacques Greilsamer & Bertrand Azema

Toys of Nuremburg: Schoenner's Toy Railways & Ships
(Lausanne, Switzerland, 1977)
Claude Jeanmarie

The Great Toys of George Carette (London, 1975)
Allen Levy

Les Bateaux Jouets (Paris, 1967)
Jacques Milet

Toys (London, 1968)
Patrick Murray

Märklin 1895-1914 (London, 1983)
Charlotte Parry-Crooke (ed)

The Art of the Tin Toy (London, 1976)
David Pressland

The Swapmeet & Toy Fair Catalogue of British Diecast Model
Toys (Felixstowe, 1984)
John Ramsay (compiler)

The Golden Age of Toys (Lausanne, Switzerland, 1967)
Jac Remise & Jean Fondin

Dinky Toys & Modelled Miniatures (London, 1981)
Mike & Sue Richardson

History of French Dinky Toys 1933-1978 (Paris, 1978)
Jean-Michel Roulet

Model Cars and Road Vehicles (London, 1983)
Patrick Trench

Mechanical Tin Toys in Colour (Dorset, 1977)
Arno Weltens

The catalogues issued by toymakers are of great value to the collector as a source of information, particularly for correct dating, as well as being attractive and collectable items in their own right. As well as illustrating the toys, catalogues usually list sizes and prices and often given information on mechanical capabilities. Early toymakers' catalogues are now of considerable value, and even the more modern examples, like those illustrated here, are increasingly hard to find in good condition.

1 A spread from the colour catalogue issued in 1976 by Solido, France, publicising the maker's range of diecast transport toys. The models illustrated are (top to bottom, left page, right page) Removal

Lorry, maker's reference number (MRN) 383; Refrigerator Lorry, MRN 382; Roads Department Lorry, MRN 379; Transport Canvas Lorry, MRN 384; Trailer Lorry, MRN 388 (with Trailer, MRN 389, shown as a separate item); Horse Box Truck, MRN 385. Note that the names of the models are given in French, English and German.
2 The cover of the "Dinky Toys et Dinky Supertoys" catalogue issued by Dinky Toys, France, in 1959. The artwork is notably more "impressionistic" than that of the later catalogues on this spread.
3 A spread from the colour catalogue issued by Dinky Toys, France, in 1971; the pages shown feature highway maintenance and construction equipment and accessories, including road signs.

Just visible on the left, see also (4), is a battery-operated traffic light. The reference numbers and dimensions are given for each model. The collector should note that the colour artwork of such catalogues, whether issued by Dinky Toys or other makers, is not always to be taken as a sure guide to the finish of the models: non-existent colour schemes or shades may sometimes appear. Even photographs are sometimes re-touched in such a way as to give a misleading impression of the model's actual appearance.
4 A spread from the large-format colour catalogue issued by Dinky Toys, France, in 1970-71. The names of the models, which are shown both in colour artwork and in line drawings with dimensions,

are in French only. The working traffic light mentioned at (3) is fully visible here (top left).
5 A spread from the colour catalogue issued by Dinky Toys, France, in 1966. As noted at (2), the colour artwork in this earlier example is less sharp and detailed than in later catalogues. It is interesting to compare the illustration of the Citroen ID 19 Ambulance (FDT No 556), shown on the left, with the appearance of the model itself, shown at (13), *pages 92-93*.
6 A spread from the colour catalogue issued by Dinky Toys, Great Britain, in 1974. The pages shown are largely devoted to dramatic publicity for the "big" "new" Atlas Digger (DT No 984) which was issued in 1974 and was in production until 1979.
7 The cover of the colour catalogue

issued by Dinky Toys, Great Britain, in 1961: a most attractive design. It is marked "U.K. 9th Edition" (the catalogues issued between 1952 and 1964 were styled as "1st Edition" to "12th Edition") and was priced at 2d (1p, 1c). The first catalogue in which Dinky Toys models were shown was issued by Meccano Ltd in 1934-35; the last appeared in 1978-79, shortly before production ceased at the Liverpool factory.

8 The cover of the colour catalogue issued by Dinky Toys, France, in 1962. Like the slightly earlier example shown at (2), the artwork is in an "impressionistic" style. Traces of the inked stamp added by the retailer who distributed this particular example can be seen in the lower right corner, in the

rectangle that was printed on the cover for this purpose.

9 A spread from the large black-and-white catalogue issued by Meccano Ltd, Great Britain, in 1938-39. The pages shown are devoted to the maker's Aeroplane Constructor Outfits, featuring the nut-and-bolt assembly of the metal parts with which the "Meccano" name is synonymous. These constructor kits were issued from 1931 until the outbread of World War II, and ranged in size from the basic "Number 00" outfit, priced at 3s 3d (16½p, 20c) in the mid-1930s, to the "Number 2 Special", priced at £1 2s 6d (£1.12½, $1.35), from which aircraft of several types could be constructed. The parts were normally finished in blue-and-white, but grey and camouflage

finishes appeared towards the end of the 1930s. As indicated at the bottom of the right-hand page of the spread shown here, a clockwork motor to power wheels and propellers could be purchased as a separate item.

10 A spread from the colour catalogue issued in 1963 by Lesney Products Ltd, Great Britain. The left-hand page is devoted to the maker's "King Size" diecast models. The smaller "1-75" series toys, with which the "Matchbox" brand name is chiefly associated, feature on the right-hand page, where one of the plastic garages issued from 1959 onwards is shown, along with vehicles and items from the maker's various "Accessory Packs".

11 A spread from a colour catalogue issued in the 1970s by Solido,

France. The pages shown illustrate the maker's range of diecast fire appliances in 1:55 scale, stressing the fact that the "Tonergam" models produce an engine sound when pushed along. A number of the models illustrated here are shown in actuality on *page 98-99*.

12 A spread from the colour catalogue issued for the French market by Corgi Toys, Great Britain, in 1979. Note that here, as in the similar item shown at (13), the models are illustrated with photographs rather than colour artwork.

13 A spread from the colour catalogue issued for the French market by Corgi Toys, Great Britain, in 1973. Under the heading "Corgi au secours" ("Corgi to the rescue"), a selection of appropriate vehicles is shown in colour photographs.

1 Box for Ford Highway Patrol Car by Ichiko, Japan; dating from around 1958. The front of the lid bears an attractive colour picture of the car, a statement of its special features, and the maker's slogan— "Quality First Toy of Ichiko"—and serial number. The side of the lid, uppermost in the photograph, repeats the statement of special features and illustrates the "moving warning light" with a line drawing. The car itself is shown at (3), *pages 58-59*: it is fairly typical of the middle-range Japanese tinplate toys of the period, with much printed detail (in this case with police lettering and badges), "Ford" numberplates at front and rear, and bright metal bumpers, radiator, windscreen frame and side-mounted trim strips. Tinted plastic windows are fitted at

front and rear and it has a printed interior with the maker's trademark on the top of the rear seat. The wheels are rubber, with metal discs printed with whitewalls and hub-caps. Friction drives the rear wheels, producing a siren sound and, via a crank, causing the roof-mounted warning light to revolve. Length of car: 9·375in (23·81cm).

2 Box for Truck by "AW", USSR; dating from around 1960. Like the toy it holds, this is a fairly solid and utilitarian piece of packaging; the rather fanciful illustration on the Cyrillic-lettered lid, featuring elves and bunny-rabbits, hardly matches the model—shown at (4), *pages 48-49*—which is of tabbed-and-slotted heavy-gauge tinplate, clockwork-powered, and looks well-suited to hard work down on the

old collective farm! Length of truck: 12·75in (32·385cm).

3 Box for Mechanical Digger by Gama, West Germany; dating from around 1957. This toy is of considerable interest in that it was made in five or more different versions in the late 1950s; the initial model was constructed entirely of tinplate, but in subsequent versions increasing amounts of plastic were used. This box contains the model with the maker's serial number 2808; this model, which is shown at (4), *pages 60-61,* has a cab of tough plastic. Also illustrated on the box are the models with the serial numbers 280 and 2806; an earlier model in the series, serial number 282, dating from around 1956 and made of heavy-gauge tinplate throughout, is shown at

(3), *pages 60-61.* To the left of the box lid, a series of drawings shows how levers on the cab control the actions of the digger's bucket. To the right of the top drawing, a "deleted" key indicates that there is no need for winding, the toy being battery-powered. Overall length of toy: 16in (40·64cm).

4 Bristol Bulldog Airplane by Straco, Japan; dating from 1958-59. Both the box and the toy itself are shown here, the latter disassembled; the toy is shown assembled at (7), *pages 114-115.* This yellow cantilever-wing monoplane displays artistic licence in both name and finish: the Bristol Bulldog was a biplane fighter aircraft of the 1930s, and this model is in civilian livery but with roundels that combine British and French military

markings! In tabbed-and-slotted tinplate, with a well-detailed pressed-tin radial engine, a plastic propeller and rubber wheels, it is battery-powered, with stop-and-go action and a turning propeller. As shown here, it is made in three parts — fuselage, mainplane and tailplane — with the method of assembly illustrated on the side of the lid. Length of aircraft: 12in (30·48cm); wingspan: 14·5in (36·83cm).

5 Remote-Control Satellite by Arnold, West Germany; dating from late 1957. This fascinating toy appeared on the market within a few days of the worldwide sensation caused by the successful flight of the Soviet "Sputnik 1" on 4 October 1957: an excellent illustration of the way in which enterprising toymakers must keep abreast of real-life

developments. The box bears a striking illustration of the satellite whirling through space; the toy itself, shown at (7), *pages 116-117,* is of pressed tin, with plastic vanes and aerials. It is a "flying toy" powered by Arnold's ingenious remote-control system: the toy is attached to a pressed-tin handset by a coiled-wire cable — in this case 31in (78·74cm) long — consisting of an outer layer, which revolves when the crank on the handset is turned, and an inner non-revolving core. The harder the handset is cranked, the higher and faster the toy flies: it can be made to alter course, climb or dive by altering the angle at which the handset is held, and can be made to fly backwards by cranking the handle in reverse.

6 Box for Twin-Engined Airliner by Tipp and Company, West Germany; dating from 1956. The box features an illustration of the prototype — in KLM livery and bearing the legend "The Flying Dutchman" along its upper fuselage (with "De Vliegende Hollander" on the other side) — in an airport setting, and displays also the maker's trademark and the serial number "58F". The toy itself, shown at (3), *pages 114-115,* is of good-quality tinplate, with plastic propellers, and has a detachable wing section. It is friction-driven. Length of aircraft: 9·75in (24·765cm); wingspan: 12·375in (31·43cm).

7 Fire Engine by "K", Japan; dating from 1958-59. Both the box and the toy itself are shown here; another view of the toy is shown at

(1), *pages 56-57.* As in the case of the Japanese-made car at (1) above, the box both states the special features of the toy and illustrates them. Of quite good-quality tinplate, the toy has a wealth of printed detail and the usual bright-metal fittings. It is friction-driven (front wheels) and a siren noise is produced as it moves. The major feature is illustrated on the side of the box: when the lever visible just behind the cab is pushed in the direction indicated, the gilt metal bell in the centre of the body begins to ring, the three-section ladder unfolds and extends to its full length of 27in (68·58cm), and a small pressed-tin fireman (until then invisible) springs erect at its upper end. Length of toy: 13in (33·02cm).

All the toys shown on this spread are from the collection of Ron McCrindell, Sidmouth, Devon.

1 "Huntley & Palmers" Biscuit Tin Bus, made by Huntley, Bourne & Stevens, Reading, Great Britain; dating from 1929. Although it is a fairly accurate model of a six-wheeled London "General" omnibus of its time, this has a splendid "toy-like" quality. Made for a leading British biscuit maker, it bears the registration number "1929": it is safe to assume that this is its date, and that it was marketed, full of biscuits, around Christmas of that year. On the back of the toy is a small "HB&S Ltd" trademark: the tin-box manufacturer Huntley, Bourne & Stevens made many containers for Huntley & Palmers.

The bus is beautifully lithographed, the passengers being different on either side, and, most unusually for a biscuit-tin toy, it has a small clockwork motor. Biscuit tin novelties are very collectable and some items, like this bus, which was probably only made for a brief time at Christmas 1929, are now both rare and usually expensive. Length: 9·5in (24·13cm).

2 Gauge "1" "Municipal Tramways" Tramcar by Bing, Nuremburg, Germany; a lithographed tinplate toy dating from around 1906. This example has an electric motor; the toy was also available in clockwork and was made in Gauge "0". The old-style white-backed torch bulbs that form the working headlights are clearly visible. The terracotta passengers on the top deck are

figures made by Märklin, Germany, to complement Gauge "1" trains. Bing's trams seem to have been made in small numbers in comparison with the maker's trains, and they are now rare: as is often the case, the Gauge "0" versions are the hardest to find. Length: 9·75in (24·765cm).

3 Taxi by Lehmann, Germany; dating from 1906. This is a charming little toy which, possibly because of its archaic "horseless carriage" appearance, does not appear to have been in production later than 1910; thus, although Lehmann toys were made in large numbers, this particular model is rare. It is powered by a simple coiled-wirespring mechanism. Length: 5·25in (13·3cm).

4 "Express" Van by an unidentified

German maker; a simple "penny toy", dating from the mid-1920s but in a long tradition of cheaply-made lithographed tinplate toys going back to the 1890s. Early "penny toys" are now rare and expensive, but later specimens like this one are not too hard to find. Length: 5in (12·7cm).

5 Steam Roller by Günthermann, Nuremburg, Germany; dating from around 1910. This lithographed tinplate toy is fitted with the forward-and-backward, automatically operating clockwork mechanism found on most toy steam rollers. Length: 8in (20·32cm).

6 Steam Roller by Doll et Cie, Nuremburg, Germany; dating from around 1928. Made by a firm that specialised in steam-powered models, this spirit-fired steam roller

3

7

11

9 10

12

is driven by a single piston-valve cylinder and has slip-eccentric reversing gear. The brass boiler is fitted with a safety-valve, whistle, pressure- and water-gauges and lubricator. Although in somewhat shabby condition, it is in working order. Length 13in (33·02cm).
7 Mamod Steam Wagon by Mamod (Malins Ltd), Great Britain; the only item shown on this spread that is still in production and remains available in toyshops. This massive model, with a pleasing resemblance to its Foden prototype, is somewhat underpowered, with a single oscillating cylinder. The steam wagon has been in production since the mid-1970s; originally a spirit-fired model, it is now fired by Meta-type solid-fuel tablets. Length: 16in (40·64cm).

8 "Also" Delivery Car by Lehmann, Germany; Numbered "700",this was first patented in 1908 and was in the maker's catalogue until the 1920s. An attractive tinplate toy, it is powered by Lehmann's favoured coiled-spring clockwork mechanism, and has its front wheels set to steer in a circle. Like most toys by Lehmann, it was marketed in large numbers over a long period and so should not be too hard to find; however, Lehmann toys have now become fashionable among collectors, and, consequently, expensive. Length 4in (10·16cm).
9 Autobus by Lehmann, Germany; an item in production in the period c1910-1930. Numbered "590", this is a most attractive toy, with the usual Lehmann coiled-spring

mechanism and with rack-and-pinion steeering. It is now very desirable, especially to bus collectors, and despite being made over a long period is rare in the mint condition shown here. Length: 8·25in (20·9cm).
10 Fire Engine by G.G. Kellerman & Company, Nuremburg, Germany; a "penny toy" dating from the mid-1920s. It is unpowered and bears the maker's "CKO" trademark. Such items should not be too hard to find, nor too expensive. Length: 5·5in (13·97cm).
11 Fire Engine by Johann Distler, Nuremburg, Germany; dating from c1920, this bears the maker's "JDN" and globe trademark. It is a most pleasing tinplate toy, clockwork-powered, with a bell that sounds as it runs along and

an operating ladder. Although provision is made for six firemen, no example has been found with that number; nor was it catalogued with more than four figures. It was also available with working head-lights and an "automatic" garage. Length of chassis: 9·5in (24·13cm).
12 Biscuit Tin Delivery Van; this item is almost certainly of British manu-facture and dates from the World War I period. Although this nicely-lithographed tinplate toy, with embossed figures at front and sides, comes under the general heading of "biscuit tins", it may have originally contained tea. Such biscuit tin toys are now highly collectable, particularly when they represent wheeled vehicles—see also (1)—and fetch high prices. Length:5·5in (13·97cm).

Tinplate Lorries and Vans by European Makers, 1930s-1950s

1 Renault-Type Tipping Lorry by C. Rossignol, Paris, France; dating from 1937-39. This toy bears no maker's mark but is fairly confidently attributed to Rossignol on stylistic grounds. With a painted finish in mottled red-and-fawn, it is fitted with a simple tipping rear body with a hinged tailboard. The chassis has pressed side-members. The two-piece wheels are of pressed tin and a clockwork motor drives the rear pair. A limited item. Length: 7·125in (18·0975cm).

2 Articulated Lorry by an unidentified British maker—it has "Made in England" printed along the tops of the mudguards—dating from c1946-50. This simple lorry of tabbed-and-slotted tinplate construction, with pressed and printed details, is possibly the work of the Mettoy Company Limited. A clockwork motor concealed within the cab, with a permanently-fixed winder protruding from the left central chassis, drives the rear pair of two-piece printed-tin wheels on the cab unit. Fairly common. Length: 9·06in (23·012cm).

3 Tipping Lorry by an unidentified British maker—note that it has "Made in England" printed on the side of the cab—dating from c1935-40. This model of a forward-control lorry (the term is used of a cab without a bonnet) has a simple tipping rear body with pressed detail simulating planked sides. The tailboard is fixed. A clockwork motor with a permanently-fixed winder drives the rear wheels. Note the printed "Dunlop Fort" tyres. This is a fairly common item.

Length: 7·68in (19·507cm).

4 "Games" Delivery Van by Chad Valley, Great Britain; this example dating from c1946. The Chad Valley "Games Van" so called because of the many games by the maker illustrated on its roof and upper sides, was one of the most attractive tinplate vans produced in Britain in the 1930s-40s. It is fitted with a "Dennis" radiator and has the numberplate "CV 10032" above its nicely-printed bonnet. The sides bear the company's name and its Royal Warrant, with crest and "By Appointment . . ." legend. The van is fitted with an opening rear door and a flat-spring clockwork motor drives its rear wheels. This very popular model is scarce, but easier to find than the very similar toy shown at (5).

· Length: 9·75in (24·765cm).

5 "Crumpsall Cream Crackers" Delivery Van by Chad Valley, Great Britain; dating from c1938. The same pressing as (4), but with an appropriate finish, this was produced as a novelty biscuit tin (to function as a toy when emptied) for the Co-Operative Wholesale Society; note the "CWS" monograms among the wealth of printed detail. Its rear wheels are driven by a clockwork motor that has a wire spring; this was to allow the biscuit compartment to have a flat base. A fairly scarce item. Length: 9·75in (24·765cm).

6 Tipping Lorry by an unidentified British maker; dating from c1948-52. In lightweight tinplate, with a tin driver, this has a lever-operated tipping rear body that is held in

place by twisted tabs (one is visible in the photograph). It has a pressed chassis with running-boards and is fitted with two-piece printed wheels, the rear pair clockwork-driven. It is fairly typical of the low-priced tinplate toys made in Britain in the 1930s-50s. Fairly common. Length: 9·875in (25·0825cm).

7 Tipping Lorry by Camtoy, Great Britain; dating from c1948. This model of a forward-control lorry has fully-printed details, including windows, with the numberplate "PT 668". Its tipping rear body is held in place by turned-over tabs and it has two-piece printed wheels. This is a fairly common item. Length: 6·75in (17·145cm).

8 Push-Along Lorry by an unidentified maker; dating from the 1940s. It bears what appears to be an "S/F"

trademark on the cab doors. Constructed of lightweight tinplate, it has printed details that include bonnet ventilators, and it is fitted with two-piece pressed-tin wheels. Limited. Length: 7·25in (18·415cm).

9 Light Truck by Paya, Spain; dating from c1940. This cheaply-made toy of lightweight tinplate has a clockwork motor that drives the rear wheels. Note the maker's trademark printed to the rear of the cab door; the cab incorporates the tinplate silhouette figure of a driver. This is a fairly limited item. Length: 7·58in (19·253cm).

10 "Colis Express" Delivery Van by Memo, France; dating from c1945-50. Note the maker's trademark on the door of this lightweight tinplate toy with its rather pleasing printed details. The

pressed-tin radiator was probably used by the maker on several other models. A clockwork motor, with an over-length permanently-fixed winder protruding from the base on the left side, drives the rear wheels. It is fairly common. Length: 5·75in (14·605cm).

11 "Express Delivery" Van by Wells, Great Britain; note that "British Made" is printed along the bottom of the radiator. This tinplate toy dates from c1935, although it has a considerably earlier appearance. The maker produced the same model in the finish of the "Carter Paterson" haulage company. A limited item. Length: 4·75in (12·065cm).

12 "Express Transport" Van by Wells, Great Britain—with "Made in England" printed on the front doors

—dating from c1947. Of tabbed-and-slotted tinplate, this toy is fitted with printed perforated-disc wheels, the rear pair driven by a clockwork motor with a permanently-fixed winder. This is a limited item. Length: 7·25in (18·415cm).

13 "Express Road Transport" Van by Burnett, Great Britain; dating from c1950. Established in Birmingham before World War I, Burnett Limited moved to London around 1914 and later became part of the Chad Valley company. This example of a Burnett toy is an extremely simple pressing in lightweight tinplate, with basic printed detail. A clockwork motor with a permanently-fixed winder drives the rear wheels, which are of two-piece pressed tin. This is an item of limited availability. Length: 5·875in (14·923cm).

1 "Shell" and "BP" Articulated Petrol Tanker by an unidentified British maker, dating from the 1940s. In view of the similarities in pressing and dimensions between this model —see also (2)—and that shown at (3), which is certainly by Mettoy, we may safely say that this is probably the work of Mettoy. It is of tabbed-and-slotted tinplate construction, with "Shell" printed on the left side of the tank, "BP" on the right, and the legend "Shell-Mex B.P. Ltd" on the cab doors, with crest, and over the radiator. The number "7756", probably the maker's reference number, is also printed on the cab door. Among the other well-printed details are filler caps, a ladder on the left rear side of the tank, and tyre-tread and hub details on the six pressed-tin wheels. The

rear wheels of the tractor unit are driven by a simple clockwork motor with a permanently-fixed winder that protrudes at the left centre of its chassis. A fairly common item. Length: 7·87in (19·989cm).
2 "Esso" Articulated Petrol Tanker by an unidentified British maker—it has "Made in England" printed along the tops of both front mudguards —dating from the 1940s. This is of the same tabbed-and-slotted tinplate construction as (1), and the rear wheels of the cab unit are driven by a simple clockwork motor with a permanently-fixed winder that protrudes at the centre left of the chassis. Its printed detail includes "Esso" on both sides of the tank, filler caps, radiator and headlights (pressed out a little), and tyre treads and hubs on its six pressed-

tin wheels. Again, as at (1), with regard to the similarities in pressing and dimensions between this and the model at (3), it is possible that this toy also is the work of Mettoy, perhaps made specially for marketing by another wholesaler or for sale through special retail outlets. It is a fairly common item. Length: 7·87in (19·989cm).
3 "International Oil" Articulated Petrol Tanker by Mettoy Company Limited, Great Britain; dating from the 1940s. This toymaking company was established in 1934 by a refugee from Germany, the dispossessed owner of the well-known German maker Tipp and Company, Nuremburg. Mettoy established a reputation for its relatively cheap tinplate clockwork toys in the immediate pre-War

period—and was eventually to become the "parent" company of the famous Corgi Toys range of diecast models, shown elsewhere in this book. On this model, Mettoy's trademark appears above the printed radiator, while the legend "Made in England" is printed along the tops of the front mudguards. The pressing and dimensions closely resemble those of the models shown at (1) and (2), which we have thus tentatively ascribed to Mettoy. The printed details include "International Oil" and logo on the tank sides, the legends "Capacity 800 Gallons" and "Highly Inflammable" on the lower part of the tank, filler caps and cab doors. The wheels are printed tinplate with plain tyres; a clockwork motor with a permanently-fixed

winder drives the rear wheels of the tractor unit. This is a limited item. Length: 7·87in (19·989cm).

4 "Pool" Articulated Petrol Tanker by Mettoy, Great Britain; dating from the 1940s. Again with the maker's trade-mark above the radiator and "Made in England" printed on the tops of the mudguards, this tabbed-and-slotted, clockwork-driven tinplate model has a suitably austere wartime finish, in drab grey with white details. "Pool" petrol represented the output in the 1940s of the major petroleum companies, which, in Britain, "pooled" their resources in wartime. Note also that the mudguards of this vehicle are finished in white: it was a common practice in wartime Britain to have the extremities of vehicles painted white, in an

attempt to lessen the hazards of driving on dimmed and shielded lights in the anti-air raid "blackouts" of the period. A fairly limited item. Length: 7·87in (19·989cm).

5 Renault-Type Petrol Tanker by C. Rossignol, Paris, France; dating from the years immediately before World War II. Although it lacks such details as mudguards and head-lamps, this model, of lightweight tinplate construction, has a pressed-tin chassis with simulated springing and a pressed filler cap that is fixed to the top of the tank by tab-and-slot. Its printed details include the legend "Essence Pour Automobiles/Shell" on the sides of the tank, a petrol can on the cab door, and a bonnet securing-catch. Overall, it has a most pleasing "toy-like" quality and is most

attractively coloured. The two-piece tinplate wheels are single-sided; the rear pair are driven by a clockwork motor with a permanently-fixed winder (note its folding top) protruding at the right rear of the chassis. The Rossignol company, founded by Charles Rossignol in the 1860s, had established a reputation with its "carpet toy" trains by the turn of the century. Between World Wars I and II, the maker produced cheap ranges of clockwork and electric trains in Gauge "0" and, in the 1920s, began to make road vehicles, including a range of Paris buses, continuing in production until the early 1960s. This is an item of fairly limited availability. Length: 8·17in (20·752cm).

6-7 "Campsa" Petrol Tanker by Rico, Alicante, Spain; dating from the

1940s. Note the maker's "R.S.A." trademark and wagon motif printed on the cab door of this simple model in lightweight tinplate, and, at (6), the repetition of the "R.S.A." mark in large letters at the rear of the tank. It is fitted with perforated disc wheels of pressed tin. Printed details include "Campsa" on the sides of the tank, filler caps, hoses on the lower sides of the tank, and mudguards. The rear wheels are driven by a clockwork motor with a permanently-fixed winder which, as can be seen at (7), protrudes from the lower rear of the chassis. The Rico company was in production with tinplate vehicles, aeroplanes and novelty toys both before and after World War II. This is a limited item. Length: 7·09in (18·009cm).

The small clockwork models made by Tri-ang (Lines Brothers Limited), Great Britain, under the "Minic" name formed a very successful alternative to the diecast models of Dinky Toys. They were in production from the mid-1930s until World War II, and again post-War into the 1950s: of more than one hundred different models produced, most were commercial vehicles, as seen here and on *pages 42-43*. All are of tabbed-and-slotted tinplate.

1 "London Transport" Double-Deck Bus; a pre-World War II Minic model, dating from around 1938. It has a detailed interior, with wooden seats and a metal steering column and wheel. It bears decals advertising "Ovaltine" on the left upper side and "Bisto" on the right

upper side and at the rear, where the number plate "AYV 604" is fitted. Its destination board is for route number "177", with a full list of staging points from Kingsway to Mitcham. The clockwork motor drives the front pair of wheels, which are of tinplate and are fitted with white rubber tyres. This is a scarce item. Length: 7·1875in (183mm).
2 "London Transport" Double-Deck Bus; the same model as (1), but finished in more familiar London Transport red, with the grey roof normally seen on pre-World War II London double-deckers. A scarce item. Length: 7·1875in (183mm).
3 "London Transport" Double-Deck Bus; a post-World War II example, dating from around 1948. Construction is as (1), but interior detail is less and the advertising

decals have changed: "Ovaltine" is on the right side and "Bovril" on the left. The destination board is unchanged. It is finished in London Transport's post-War red-and-cream livery and is fitted with black rubber tyres. A limited item. Length: 7·1875in (183mm).
4 "London Transport" Double-Deck Bus; a later example than (3), dating from around 1950. Construction is still as (1-3), but both details and wheels have changed. The cream finish is restricted to the upper deck; the advertising decals are for "Penguin" models on the left "Minic" on the right and "Tri-ang Toys" at the rear; the numberplate "LBL 174" is fitted (these letters were used by *L*ines *B*rothers *L*imited on many models!); and the destination board is for route number "14",

from King's Cross to Putney. It has cast metal wheels fitted with black rubber balloon tyres. Limited. Length: 7·1875in (183mm).
5 "London Transport" Double-Deck Bus; dating from around 1953. Most details are as (4), but the cream finish is now reduced to a narrow strip around the bottom of the upper deck and the overall red finish extends to the mudguards, black on all earlier models. The decals advertise "Tri-ang Pedal Motors" (left), "Pedigree Dolls" (right), and "Frog" and "Penguin" models at the rear—all Lines Brothers ranges. A limited item. Length: 7·1875in (183mm).
6 "Green Line" Single-Deck Bus; dating from around 1950. For this model, Tri-ang used the chassis and lower deck of the double-decker

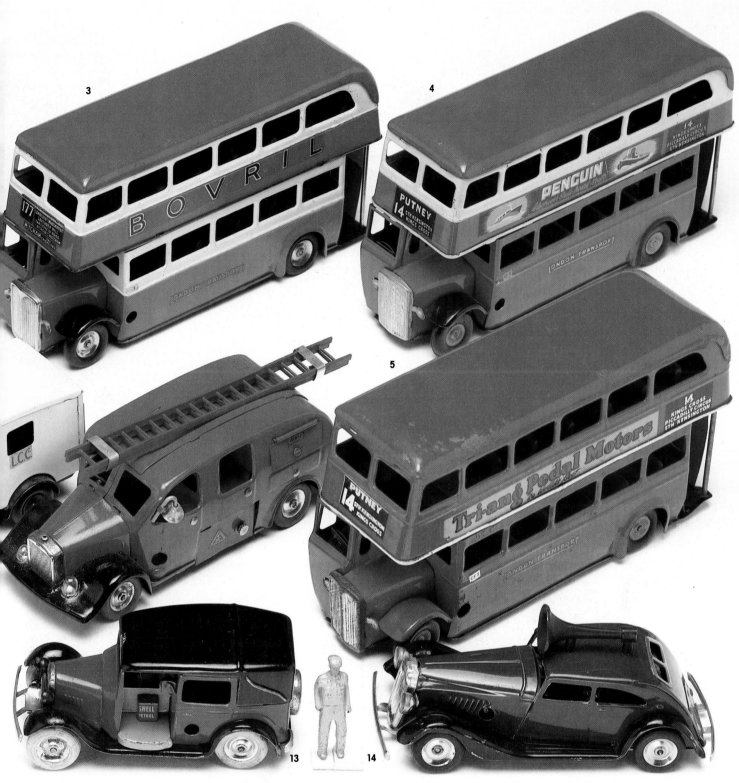

(1-5), with a pressed-tin roof. The destination board is for "Dorking", and decals at the rear, where the numberplate "LBL 174"—the same as (4)—is fitted, advertise "Frog" and "Penguin" models. A limited item. Length: 7·1875in (183mm).

7 "L.C.C." Ambulance; dating from around 1954. This model of a forward control vehicle was produced only in the post-World-War-II period. It has plastic wheels fitted with black rubber balloon tyres; a clockwork motor concealed within the cab drives the front pair of wheels. Note the raised "Ambulance" sign on the roof; it also bears Red Cross and "L.C.C." (London County Council) decals. This is of limited availability. Length: 4·875in (124mm).

8 Fire Engine; dating from around 1939. This pre-War model features battery-powered headlights (the bulbs only can be seen here: the tin cowls originally fitted are missing); it reappeared without working lights in the post-War period. It is provided with a bell and a detachable two-stage ladder and has opening side-hatches for the hose- and battery-storage compartments. Note also the well-modelled radiator. This is a scarce item. Length: 6·375in (162mm).

9 Traction Engine and Trailer; dating from around 1952. The engine has a tinplate body and is fitted with a brass front cover, chimney and valve cover. The simple trailer also has a tinplate body, and both vehicles are fitted with large and rather unconvincing black plastic wheels. This model is limited.

Length overall: 8·875in (225mm).

10 Steam Roller; dating from around 1950. This model has a tinplate body with a brass filler cap (in fact, the securing nut for the steerable front roller), chimney and valve cover. The roller and wheels are of grey plastic and, as at (9), tend to detract from the otherwise pleasing appearance of the model. The clockwork mechanism is geared to give alternate forward and reverse movement. This is a limited item. Length: 5·125in (130mm).

11 London Taxi Cab; dating from around 1950. This very well-detailed model, complete with tinplate bumpers, a "For Hire" sign and taxi-meter, a "Taxi" sign on the roof, plastic-lensed headlights, and a spare-wheel cover at the rear, has a clockwork motor that drives the

rear wheels. It is a limited item. Length: 4·125in (105mm).

12-13 London Taxi Cab; dating from around 1938. The two examples shown, (12) finished in dark blue and (13) in red, with a black roof and rear canopy in both cases, are of the same construction as (11). These pre-War models have grey floors and spare "Shell Petrol" cans. They are limited items. Length: 4·134in (105mm).

14 Traffic Control Car; dating from around 1948. This model of a Vauxhall police vehicle was the only Minic model reissued after World War II to retain a diecast driver and passenger. It is fitted with a single roof-mounted loudspeaker and has headlights that are soldered to their supports. A limited item. Length: 5·125in (130mm).

1 Breakdown Lorry; dating from c1938. This was the only model in the "Minic" range of clockwork-powered vehicles of tabbed tinplate to be fitted with two clockwork motors: one to drive the front wheels in the usual way, the other to raise and lower the hook on the tinplate jib, an operation controlled by a lever engaging on a cog. The angle of the jib can be altered by use of the crank-handle on the nearside rear—just visible in the model shown at (3). A positive stop/start control for the vehicle is also fitted. The pre-World-War-II example shown here is distinguished by its tinplate wheels with white rubber tyres, by the spare petrol can (not visible in the photograph) mounted on the nearside running-board, and by its early-type "Minic" and "Tri-ang" decals on the sides. Scarce. Length: 6·25in (159mm).

2 Breakdown Lorry; dating from c1954. The details of construction and mechanism are as (1), but this post-War model has later-type decals, front mudguards that are painted rather than plated, and plastic wheels with black rubber balloon tyres. It is a limited item. Length: 6·25in (159mm).

3 Breakdown Lorry; dating from c1950 (when one of the authors was given the example shown here as a birthday present!). Construction and mechanism are as (1-2), but this is the intermediate-type model, with large decals of pre-War size, plated front mudguards and cast metal wheels. A limited item. Length: 6·25in (159mm).

4 "L.N.E.R." Van; dating from c1946-48. In the immediate post-War period, using van pressings of pre-War type, Tri-ang produced delivery vans in the colours of the four regional railway companies of the pre-nationalisation period. The L.N.E.R. (London and North-Eastern Railway) version shown here carries "Express Parcels Service" decals and "Tri-ang Pedal Motors" stickers. It is fitted with opening rear doors with a locking-bar and has tinplate wheels of pre-War type. A limited item. Length: 5·625in (143mm).

5 "L.M.S." Van; dating from c1946-48. The same model as (4), but in L.M.S. (London, Midland and Scottish Railway) colours and with a sticker advertising "Tri-ang Dolls' Houses". Limited. Length: 5·625in (143mm).

6 "Southern Railway" Van; dating from c1946-48. As (4) and (5), but in S.R. green and with a sticker advertising "Penguin" aircraft. Limited. Length: 5·625in (143mm).

7 Carter Paterson Delivery Van; dating from c1938. The body and chassis are as (4-6), but this pre-War model has plated mudguards, a petrol can on the nearside running-board and white rubber tyres. Scarce. Length: 5·625in (143mm).

8 Mechanical Horse and Pantechnicon; dating from c1938. This uses the same pre-War-type cab pressing as (1). On this pre-War example, the model is steered via an adjustable rear axle on the Horse and an adjustable front axle on the Pantechnicon. In post-War models, the Pantechnicon had no front wheels and was mounted directly on to the Horse,

as seen at (17). A scarce item. Length: 7·75in (197mm).

9 Delivery Van; dating from c1938. Details are as (1-7), but this model, although of pre-War production (with its spare petrol can just visible on the nearside running-board) is fitted with black tyres. It bears "Minic Transport" decals. Limited. Length: 5·625in (143mm).

10 Shutter Van; dating from c1954. This Minic model of a forward-control van was produced only during the post-War period; note, however, that the plated radiator is the same as that used on the earlier models. A clockwork motor within the cab drives the front wheels, which are of the late type, made of plastic and fitted with black rubber balloon tyres. It bears "Minic Transport" decals. This is a limited

item. Length: 4·875in (124mm).

11 Ford Light Delivery Van; dating from c1938. The clockwork motor drives the rear wheels, which are of pressed-steel-disc-type with white rubber tyres. The chassis and bumper are a single pressing, but the radiator, without headlights, is separate. A "Shell Petrol" can is mounted on the nearside running-board and the van bears small "Minic Transport" decals. Limited. Limited. Length: 5·5in (140mm).

12 Articulated Milk Tanker; dating from c1950. This model uses the same Mechanical Horse as shown at (8), but the example shown here is of post-War type, with cast metal wheels and no spare petrol can. In fact, this Tanker appeared only during the post-War period. The tank, fitted with three filler domes

and with a hose box at the rear, bears "Minic Dairies" decals. Limited. Length: 7·00in (178mm).

13 Mechanical Horse and Watney's Barrel Trailer; dating from c1954. For this purpose of this model, a tinplate "Watney" sign was mounted at the front of the roof of the Horse and a red plastic barrel on the roof top. The Trailer is of turned wood. Length: 5·5in (140mm).

14 Dustcart; dating from c1948. The chassis and cab are as (1-7), post-War type, and the special dustcart body is fitted with six bright-plated sliding covers. It bears "Minic" and "Tri-ang" decals. Limited. Length: 5·5in (140mm).

15 Tipping Lorry; dating from c1938. The chassis and cab are as (1-7), pre-War type. The rear body, with a hinged tailboard, is manually

tipped. A limited model. Length: 5·625in (143mm).

16 Searchlight Lorry; dating from c1938. This has the standard chassis and cab of pre-War type, but with a platform body to accommodate a battery-powered searchlight and a battery-box with a hinged lid. The searchlight has an on/off screw and can be fully traversed and elevated. Limited. Length: 5·1875in (132mm).

17 Mechanical Horse and Cable-Drum Trailer; dating from c1954. The forward-control Horse is a late model, with characteristic radiator and headlights; it is fitted with a steerable rear axle. The double rear wheels of the Trailer, with plastic Cable Drums, are cast metal with balloon tyres. Limited. Length: 8·5in (216mm).

43

1 Wrecker Truck by an unidentified West German maker; dating from around 1957. The words "Made in Western Germany" are printed along the bottom of the bright metal radiator. This is a large and robust toy of heavy-gauge tinplate: a simple push-along model. The turntable-mounted crane turns through 360° and its hook is raised and lowered by means of the manually-operated crank handle at the left of its base. The headlights are plastic and the single-sided wheels are of heavy moulded plastic. Length: 15·125in (38·42cm).

2 Cement Mixer on Heavy Duty Diesel Truck by SSS International, Japan; dating from 1960-61. This large and solid toy is tinplate throughout, with the exception of grey plastic sleeves around the bonnet-mounted exhaust pipes. Note the pressed details of the radiator and cab roof, the yellow-and-black printed bumper, and the bright metal headlights and steps to the cab. The wheels (the two rear pairs double) are of rubber and are fitted with metal discs. Friction drives the rear-most pair of wheels and works from them through a worm gear to rotate the drum of the cement mixer. When a small lever set into the truck chassis just to the rear of the cab (on the side of the truck away from the camera) is depressed, a hydraulic-type ram raises the drum of the cement mixer through an angle of about 45°, as is shown in this photograph, as if to empty it of its contents. Length: 13·75in (34·925cm).

3 Remote-Control Mechanical Shovel by Gama, West Germany; dating from around 1959. The words "Made in Western Germany" are printed on the white metal arm that controls the jib; note also the maker's trademark applied to the cab door. Except for its well-modelled plastic wheels, which are fitted with heavy-treaded rubber tyres, this ingenious toy is of good-quality tinplate throughout. Batteries housed in the remote-control handset shown in the background transmit power to the rear pair of wheels of the six-wheeled truck for forward and reverse movement (controlled by the buttons on the handset) and for operation of the shovel. The plastic-housed spotlight on the roof of the truck cab lights up when

the toy is in operation. The movements of the shovel are controlled by levers on either side of the cab: a manually-operated lever to the left is used to raise or lower the jib; a remote-controlled lever to the right controls the pulley mechanism that raises, lowers, opens or closes the bucket. Length: 12in (30·48cm).

4 Remote-Control Wreck Truck by Asahi, Japan; dating from around 1961. Of tinplate throughout, save for its treaded rubber wheels with metal discs, this truck has a yellow-and-black printed bumper, bright metal radiator, gold metal head-lights, and basic pressed details. The pressed-tin handset shown beside it houses batteries that power the double rear wheels: the buttons on the handset control

forward and reverse motion; the wheel on the handset steers the truck's front wheels. The crane is traversed manually and a lever at the lower rear of the truck controls the raising and lowering of the jib. The truck bears the rear number-plate: "7343—Made in Japan". Length: 10·375in (26·35cm).

5 Remote-Control Dump Truck by Asahi, Japan; dating from around 1961. The toy is tinplate throughout and is fitted with heavy-treaded rubber wheels with metal discs. Note that its printed, pressed and bright metal details exactly resemble those of (4), by the same maker—and see also (7): all three toys appear to make use of the same cab. The remote-control system is the same as that described for (4). A red light in the exhaust column

flashes when the vehicle is moving; when it is stationary, the tipping mechanism is activated by pushing up the blue lever (just visible in the photograph) at the rear of the chassis. This truck bears the same rear numberplate as (4) and (7). Length:10·375in (26·35cm).

6 Dump Truck by Tada, Japan; dating from around 1958. This simple tinplate truck has basic bright metal details—bumper and radiator, bonnet ornament, windscreen frame—and a tabbed-in "Dump" badge on the cab doors. The word "Japan" is stamped on the base. The wheels are rubber with metal discs; the front pair are friction-driven. The tipping body is activated by a lever set on the left side of the chassis, just behind the cab. Length: 8·5in (21·59cm).

7 Remote-Control Lift Dump Truck by Asahi, Japan; dating from around 1961. All the details of the cab of this good-quality tinplate toy are identical with those of the Asahi trucks described at (4) and (5), but in this case the truck itself is six-wheeled and its remote-control system is more complex. When the blue lever situated at the rear of the chassis is pushed to the right, the buttons on the handset control forward and reverse motion, with a siren sound and a flashing light in the bonnet-mounted exhaust stack, while the wheel on the handset steers the truck's front wheels; when the blue lever is pushed to the left, the buttons are used to raise the truck body on its cleverly-jointed platform and to tip it. This quite complex mechanism

is clearly visible in the photograph. The truck has heavy-treaded rubber wheels with metal discs and, like (4) and (5), bears a rear numberplate printed with the legend "7343—Made in Japan". Length: 10·75in (27·3cm).

8 Dump Truck by T.N. (Nomura Toys), Japan; dating from around 1958. This is a simple and strongly-made toy of good-quality tinplate, with bright metal bumper and radiator, pressed details on the bonnet, and a clear plastic wind-screen. It is fitted with heavy-treaded rubber wheels with metal discs; the front wheels are friction-driven. The dumper body of the truck, with pressed-tin ribbing, is activated by a lever (visible in photograph) on the left side of the chassis. Length: 8in (20·32cm).

1 "Turnpike Line" Trailer Truck by SSS International, Japan; dating from c1961-62. This large and robust toy of heavy-gauge tinplate has few embellishments other than the winch mountings on the cab front, an exhaust stack and a bright metal windscreen frame. The cab has a printed interior, with a plastic steering wheel; a numberplate, "649—Made in Japan", is fitted at the rear of the cab unit. The trailer, articulated to the cab unit by pin-and-socket, is divided into two levels by a central tinplate "floor": both levels are provided with opening doors at the rear. The wheels are double throughout and are of single-sided, heavy-treaded rubber, with metal discs. The front wheels are friction-driven. Length: 22·5in (57·15cm).

2 Tipper Truck by an unidentified maker. People's Republic of China; dating from around 1959. Although the box in which it was marketed in Europe designates this as a "tipper truck", it does not, in fact, incorporate a tipping mechanism! It is a solidly but rather crudely made tinplate toy, with yellow plastic headlights and basic bright metal details. The wheels are rubber with metal discs; friction drives the front pair of wheels. Length: 6in (15·24cm).

3 Tipping Truck by Goso, West Germany; dating from around 1960. This tinplate truck has its maker's name stamped on the bright metal trim just below the front windows. The printed interior of the cab and the composition figure of the driver (left-hand drive) are just visible in the photograph. The tipping body of the truck, with a hinged tailgate, is activated by the lever visible at the rear of the chassis. The nicely-detailed wheels are metal, with voided hubs and pressed details on the hubcaps, and are fitted with heavy-treaded rubber tyres. Friction drives the front wheels of the truck. Length: 12·75in (32·385cm).

4 Fork-Lift Truck by "MT" (Modern Toys), Japan; dating from around 1961. This ingenious and most attractive toy is powered by batteries housed in the radiator compartment at its rear (ie. non-fork) end. A lever to the left of the steering column acts as a function control: when it is pushed forward, the lever to the right of the driver's seat is used to raise, lower or halt the lift; when it is pulled back, power is transmitted to the double front wheels (made of rubber, with metal discs) for forward or reverse motion. The lift, the maker claimed, has a maximum capacity of 14oz (400gm): a small metal stabilising-wheel is fitted to the base of the truck just forward of the front wheels. Save for the black moulded plastic floor of the driver's compartment, this strongly-made toy is tinplate throughout. The tabbed-in plaque of bright metal visible on the side bears the serial number "S-1002", and the maker's trademark and patent details are printed along the top of the seat-back, as can be seen in the photograph. Length (including lift arms): 11in (27·94cm); height of lift: 8in (20·32cm).

5 Highway Service Vehicle by Haji, Japan; dating from around 1960. This simple six-wheeled truck, with friction-driven front wheels (rubber, with metal discs), came complete with five road signs of printed tinplate (as shown). The cab sides bear tabbed-in "Highway Repair" plaques. Length: 8·5in (21·59cm).

6 Trailer Truck by CKO, West Germany; dating from around 1958. This simple toy of good-quality tinplate is clockwork-powered, with drive to the double rear wheels of the cab unit. The front wheels are steerable via the small lever seen below the front bumper. The trailer unit has a pair of small wheels (just visible in the photograph) fitted to its base: these are lowered to allow the trailer to stand level when detached

from the cab unit. The tailgate is hinged and the metal wheels are fitted with treaded rubber tyres. The maker's trademark and the serial number "396" are stamped on the base of the cab unit. Length overall: 15·5in (39·37cm).

7 Ford Automobile Carrier by Asakusa Toy, Japan; dating from around 1961. This articulated transporter is tinplate throughout and is fitted with rubber wheels with metal discs. The front wheels of the cab unit are friction-driven. As shown, the toy was sold complete with four tinplate friction-driven cars, two saloons and two estates, with basic bright metal details. A ramp slides out, as shown, from beneath the upper deck of the transporter, while the rear door of the lower deck is

hinged to open downwards to provide a lower loading ramp. Length overall: 16·5in (41·91).

8 Auto Transporter by SSS International, Japan; dating from around 1960. This is a smaller and simpler transporter than the toy at (7), in tinplate with basic bright metal details and with a non-detachable articulated trailer. The wheels are rubber with metal discs; the front pair are friction-driven. It was sold, as seen, with four push-along tinplate cars. A ramp slides out from beneath the upper deck, but there is no rear door. Length overall: 12·375in (31·43).

9 "East Wind" Pickup Truck by an unidentified maker, People's Republic of China; dating from around 1959. This tinplate truck, a rather crude pressing, has the

usual bright metal details and is friction-driven (front wheels). The front wheels are metal with rubber tyres; the rear wheels are rubber with metal discs. It bears the rear-mounted numberplate "OK 0808". Length: 6·25in (15·875cm).

10 Livestock Truck by Haji, Japan; dating from around 1958. This truck, made of fairly heavy-gauge tinplate, is fitted with rubber wheels with metal discs; the front wheels are friction-driven. The only applied details are the bright metal headlights and the tabbed-in "Live Stock" signs on the cab doors. As seen here, it was sold complete with a pressed-tin cow: this push-along toy, on rubber wheels, has a head that is loosely tabbed-in in order to produce a "nodding" action. Length: 8·25in (20·955cm).

1 Canopy Truck by "PN", West Germany; dating from around 1957. This large and solid six-wheeled lorry is of tinplate, with a PVC canopy hung on a wire that fits into holes in the corners of the truck bed. It is a fairly basic model, with some pressed details and bright metal front bumpers, radiator trim and wheel hubs. The metal wheels (the rear pair friction-driven) are fitted with heavy-treaded "Dunlop" tyres. Length: 17·5in (44·45cm).

2 Breakdown Truck with Jaguar Car by Lincoln International, Hong Kong; dating from 1958-59. The simple four-wheeled tinplate truck, with basic bright metal details, is equipped with a manually-operated, swivelling crane with a plastic hook. A swivelling spotlight originally mounted on the cab roof is missing from this example. The wheels—the front pair friction-driven and the rear pair double—are solid rubber with metal discs. The Jaguar Car is friction-driven (rear wheels) and has a towing ring beneath its front bumper. Lengths (truck): 7·5in (19·05cm); (car) 5·875in (14·92cm).

3 Tipping Trailer Truck by SSS International, Japan; dating from 1961-62. This large and robust toy of heavy-gauge tinplate is articulated by a simple pillar-and-socket. On the forward left side (away from camera) of the trailer unit is a lever which, when pushed forward, causes the spring-loaded trailer body to tip with a realistic sound. The front pair of wheels of the cab unit is friction-driven; all the wheels, double throughout, are of heavy-treaded rubber with metal discs. The cab has a printed interior with a plastic steering wheel. Both units bear the rear number-plate "649"; the words "Made in Japan" are stamped on the trailer rear. Length overall: 20in (50·8cm).

4 Truck by "ΛW", USSR; dating from around 1960. A very solid toy of heavy-gauge tinplate, this has removable truck body sides (one removed for photogaph) and tailgate, utilising a rather crude tab-and-slot system. The cab has clear plastic windows, opening doors and an operating steering wheel (left-hand drive). The radiator and bumper are bright metal and the headlights plastic. The wheels are metal (note the maker's Cyrillic-lettered trademark on the

bright hubs), with red walls and heavy-treaded rubber tyres. Clockwork drives the rear wheels. Length: 12·75in (32·385cm).

5 Camera Truck by Joustra, France; dating from c1961. This attractive tinplate toy represents an American-style pickup truck with a "Radio/Television" camera, complete with pressed-tin cameraman, mounted on a wheeled dolly in the truck bed. Clockwork, controlled by an on/off switch in the truck bed, drives the rear wheels; the camera is mounted on a shaft and revolves as the vehicle moves. The cab is fitted with a clear plastic windscreen and has a well-printed interior with a metal steering wheel. The wheels are plastic, with plastic whitewalls and metal discs, and are fitted with rubber tyres. Length: 11·75in (29·845cm).

6 Platform Truck by an unidentified Japanese maker; dating from *c*1960. This ingenious tinplate toy of good quality is friction-driven (front wheels). A shaft from the drive causes the plastic spotlight mounted on the cab roof to swivel as the vehicle moves. When the lever (visible in the photograph) on the right side of the chassis is depressed, a spring mechanism raises the truck bed on its jointed metal supports and activates the tipping ram gear. The tailgate is hinged. The wheels (double at the rear) are rubber, with metal discs. Length: 11in (27·94cm).

7-10 Remote-Control Four-Way Trailer Truck by Arnold, West Germany; dating from *c*1956. This most attractive toy consists of five elements: an "M.A.N. Diesel"

Cab Unit with pillar-and-socket connection to a choice of four trailers. In our photograph, the cab unit is shown at (10) with a low-sided truck-bodied trailer with a single pair of bright metal wheels. The other trailers are: (7) a plastic "Shell" petrol tanker with one pair of bright metal wheels, bright metal rails and a rubber hose; (8) a tinplate timber carrier, with wooden logs, fitted with a single pair of bright metal wheels; (9) a tinplate low-loader with two pairs of bright metal wheels, a manually-operated crane—which may also be mounted in the socket visible near the front of the truck bed of the trailer at (10), and a hinged tailboard. The toy is powered by the usual Arnold remote-control system: the line that transmits power from the

hand-set—shown off to the right of (10)—consists of an outer and an inner cable. The crank on the hand-set turns the outer cable, which joins a sprocket in the cab unit and acts through a crown-wheel and piston to impart forward or reverse motion (depending on the direction in which the crank is turned) to the plastic rear wheels of the cab unit; the inner cable, activated by the plunger on the hand-set, steers the unit. Lengths (cab unit): 4·5in (11·43cm); (trailers): (7) 6·5in (16·51cm); (8) 6in (15·24cm); (9) 9in (22·86cm); (10) 6·5in (16·51cm).

11 Dump Truck by Kang Yuan Toys, Shanghai, People's Republic of China; dating from *c*1960. A cheap, simple but not unattractive toy, driven by friction (rear

wheels). When a lever mounted on the right front chassis is pressed, the truck body tips and the tailgate opens. Note the bright metal details and the printed interior. Length: 9·5in (24·13cm).

12 "Coca-Cola" Delivery Truck by Tipp and Company, West Germany; dating from *c*1954. This is a most attractive and well-made toy in good-quality tinplate. The Volkswagen delivery truck (note the bright metal "VW" badge on the radiator) has pressed details of flooring in the truck bed and is complete with plastic trays of red and clear plastic bottles. The numberplate "TC0-020" is fitted at front and rear. The metal wheels have treaded rubber tyres; friction drives the rear pair of wheels. Length: 9in (22·86cm).

Buses and coaches are a particularly popular area of specialisation for collectors of both tinplate and diecast transport toys. This is partly because of their attractive appearance, often enhanced by advertisements, and partly because, with so many different models of various types of buses appearing over a long period, it is possible to assemble a most satisfying thematic collection with comparative ease—although perhaps not cheaply!

1 "General" Double-Deck Bus by an unidentified British maker; dating from around 1937. This model based on a "Q2-Type" vehicle, is of an unusual forward-control (ie, without a bonnet) design: it has an entrance situated near the front on the nearside (just visible in

the photograph) and, although this latter feature is obscured in the photograph, front wheels that are set back behind the driver's compartment. The overall impression is that the vehicle is back-to-front! It is fitted with battery-powered lights, with two rather crudely-fitted bulbs at the front and one at the rear. Its printed finish includes advertisements for "Bisto" on the right and "Palm Toffee" on the nearside, with a destination board for route number "25", which seems to have been a favourite with British toymakers, since it features also on the Chad Valley bus shown at (2). The wheels are of two-piece pressed-tin construction, with printed spokes and tyres; the rear wheels are clockwork-driven and the front

axle can be turned to steer the vehicle. It is a limited item.
Length: 11·00in (27·94cm).
2 "London Transport" Double-Deck Bus by Chad Valley, Great Britain; dating from around 1950. This attractive model, based on an AEC vehicle of the 1940s, was made as a novelty biscuit tin: it has a roof that lifts off and was originally filled with Carr's Biscuits. Appropriately, "Carr's Biscuits" are advertised on the right side and on the head boards, with the toy's maker "Chad Valley Toys" on the nearside. Emptied of its freight, it makes a satisfactory toy, with a well-detailed printed finish that includes destination boards for route number "25", with a list of staging points from Seven Kings to Victoria Station. The example shown has a

clockwork motor that drives the rear wheels (note the winding-shank just forward of the rear wheels); the model was also available as a push-along toy. Items like this are likely to be comparatively expensive, as they are eagerly sought by both toy collectors and collectors of tinplate containers. It is a limited item. Length: 10·00in (24·4cm).
3 "General" Double-Deck Bus by S. Günthermann, Nuremburg, Germany; dating from around 1930. Note the famous maker's "S.G." trademark on the bonnet of this 1920s-style London bus, with its outside staircase and open cab (with pressed-tin driver). It bears printed advertisements for "Ford's Automobile" (nearside), "F.L. Cailler's Chocolates" (right) and, at the rear, "Heinz Baked Beans",

"Dunlop Tyres" and "B.P.". It has a "High Street" destination board. A clockwork motor drives the rear wheels and it is fitted with simple steering via the front axle. Most tinplate toys by this maker are scarce. Length: 9·25in (23·495cm).

4 "Chad Valley" Single-Deck Bus by Chad Valley, Great Britain; dating from around 1950. Of lightweight tinplate construction, this model has a simple yet most pleasing lithographed finish, with details of the driver and passengers. The wheels are of two-piece pressed-tin construction; a clockwork motor drives the rear wheels. Length: 11·75in (29·845cm).

5 "Midland" Single-Deck Bus by Chad Valley, Great Britain; dating from around 1950. This is the same model as that shown at (4),

but in maroon "Midland" livery instead of blue-and-cream "Chad Valley" finish. In addition, this model bears the destination board "Birmingham" above its cab. The nearside of the model is shown in the photograph; note that the lithography differs from that on the right side, seen at (4), although the work is equally charming on both sides: here we see the conductor and passengers. A limited item. Length: 11·75in (29·845cm).

6 "Nifty Bus" by an unidentified German maker—it has the patent registration "D.R.P. 257554" and the word "Germany" printed along its lower body—dating from around 1930. This model has a simple but attractively-printed tinplate body (note the number "1100" in the blue panel on the side of the

bonnet; presumably the maker's reference number) and has single-sided wheels of two-piece disc type. The clockwork motor that drives the rear wheels is geared for "stop-wait-and-go" action, with a bell signal. In the example shown, the roof is a replacement item and the tinplate figures of driver and conductor that were originally fitted are missing. A scarce item. Length: 10·5in (26·67cm).

7 Volkswagen Minibus by Goso, West Germany; dating from around 1955. This has a pressed tinplate body, incorporating an opening central doors and louvred rear wings, and is fitted with perspex windows and a divided perspex windscreen. It bears the rear numberplate "B-00412". Its metal wheels are fitted with treaded

rubber tyres; a clockwork motor, with brake, drives the rear wheels and a steering system is operated via a simulated foglamp on the side of the vehicle away from the camera. It is of limited availability. Length: 7·00in (17·78cm).

8 Paris Bus by C. Rossignol, France; dating from around 1940. This is a most attractive toy of pressed and printed tinplate, very well detailed and featuring a front bumper, a tinplate driver, a roof-mounted "6" destination board, and a railed rear platform. Note the destination board printed along the side, showing staging points from Passy to Bourse. It has printed artillery-type wheels, the rear pair clockwork-driven. This is a scarce item by a long-established maker. Length: 11·75in (28·845cm).

1 Single-Deck Trolley-Bus by S. Günthermann, West Germany; dating from the 1950s. It bears the trademark of the famous Nuremburg maker, established as early as the 1870s and still in production as part of the Siemens group in the 1960s, and has the words "Made in Western Germany" printed along its lower edge towards the rear. This trolley-bus is of pressed tinplate construction with printed details, including a clerestory roof; a tinplate pantograph is mounted on the roof, and it is fitted with rubber-tyred metal wheels. A clockwork motor, fitted with a brake, drives the rear wheels, and as the vehicle moves along a fifth wheel causes a bell concealed inside it to sound. It is equipped with simple steering via the front axle. This is a limited item. Length: 12·00in (30·48cm).

2 Single-Deck Tramcar by an unidentified West German maker; dating from around 1950. This attractive model of a type of vehicle still to be seen in the streets of many European cities has a pressed tinplate body and chassis, incorporating such details as interior partitions, a gated platform at the front, a rear step and simulated springing on the wheels. Its blue-and-cream printed finish includes the number "65" at front and sides. Note the stout wire pick-up mounted on the roof and the battery-operated headlight. The clockwork motor that drives the rear wheels has a permanently-fixed winder that is just visible in the photograph, situated below the platform gate

and a little in front of the lever that operates the brake. Limited. Length: 12·00in (30·48cm).

3 Single-Deck Tramcar by a German maker—probably by Johann Distler, Nuremburg—dating from the World War I period. As its flanged wheels suggest, this model was made to run on a track: it consists of a fairly lightweight tinplate body with a clerestory roof—the roofless upper body shown in front of the model fully displays the details of its construction—mounted on a heavier four-wheeled chassis with a track-controlled mechanism. It is fitted with a diecast headlamp. Note the variation in colour finish between the complete model and the roofless body: as on the prototype vehicles, the models were of different colours to indicate

their class, since, as on trains, passengers were segregated according to the fare paid. The toy bears no maker's mark—but this is not unusual in the case of the prolific Distler output, particularly for the period from World War I onward. This is a limited model. Length: 7·5in (19·05cm).

4 Single-Deck Tramcar by S. Günthermann, Nuremburg, Germany; dating from around 1938. The maker's "S.G." trademark can be seen just above the wheels. This tinplate toy has both pressed —the central doors, raised roof and pick-up—and attractively-printed details. A clockwork motor with a permanently-fixed winder drives the pair of wheels seen on the right in this photograph of a double-ended vehicle. Limited.

Length: 8·00in (20·32cm).

5 Twin Tramcar Set by an unidentified East German maker — it is marked "Trambind 2126" — dating from the mid-1960s. This cheerful little toy was marketed with a plastic track. The roofs and chassis of the cars are made of plastic; the bodies are lightweight tinplate, with amusing printed details of passengers. In the leading tram, with its wire pick-up, is the composition figure of a driver. This seems altogether too light-hearted a toy to have come out of the German Democratic Republic! It is a limited item. Length (each car): 7·125in (18·097cm).

6 San Francisco Cable Car by an unidentified Taiwanese maker; a model of the kind currently sold in souvenir shops to tourists in the city in which, according to the

song, these "little cable cars run halfway to the stars"! This little cable car is of lightweight tinplate and bears a wealth of printed detail: "Powell & Mason Sts." on its roof-mounted destination boards; "504" and "Municipal Railway" on its sides; planked seating; destination head-boards, and more. It carries seven pressed-tin passengers — not all visible in the photograph — as well as a driver and conductor. It has eight plastic wheels and is fitted with a "push-and-go" mechanism that also sounds a bell as it moves. This is a fairly common item. Length: 7·00in (17·78cm).

7 San Francisco Cable Car; this is almost identical to (6) and is of the same origin, although (6) has a "Chif" trademark and this has only an arrow-head sign. Presumably,

the manufacture of these cheap souvenirs in Taiwan is carried out in independent workshops, each working to roughly the same specifications. This example is fractionally longer than (6), its colour finish differs, and it carries only four passengers and a driver. It is a fairly common model. Length: 7·125in (18·0975cm).

8 San Francisco Cable Car; another souvenir produced in Taiwan for sale in the USA. This is slightly smaller and less detailed than the examples at (6) and (7); the pressing lacks the rear steps of the larger models. Its roof-mounted destination board is for "Bay & Taylor Sts." Like the item at (6) and (7), it is fitted with eight plastic wheels and has a "push-and-go" mechanism with ringing bell action.

It is a fairly common item. Length: 6·625in (16·8725cm).

9 Double-Deck Tramcar by Gebrüder Bing, Nuremburg, Germany; dating from around 1930. This is a late and fairly minor product of one of the most famous of all makers of tinplate toys, whose trademark is just visible on the front of the lower deck. It is intended to run on track of 1·25in (32mm) gauge; ie, approximately Gauge "0". It is of very simple pressed tinplate construction, with a canopy (in this example, a replacement) on four metal supports, and it is fitted with four flanged wheels of cast metal. Its clockwork motor has a large permanently-fixed winder; note the wire brake-lever protruding from the rear of the underframe. Limited. Length: 6·25in (15·875cm).

1 Diesel Road Roller by an unidentified British maker; dating from around 1950. The only marks of origin on this toy are the words "Made in England" printed across its upper front. It is of pressed tinplate construction with printed details, the canopy being provided with wire supports, and is complete with the two-piece tinplate figure of a driver. An exposed clockwork motor at the rear (the large spring is just visible in the photograph), with a permanently-fixed winder, drives the rear wheels in alternate forward and reverse motion, a common feature in toy rollers; the model is steered via its swivel-mounted front roller. Fairly common. Length: 7·75in (19·685cm).

2 Diesel Road Roller by Mettoy Company Limited, Great Britain;

dating from around 1950. Made of pressed and printed tinplate, this model features an open cab with a pressed-tin seat and a cast metal steering wheel. A rear-mounted clockwork motor with a permanently-fixed winder (just visible in the photograph) drives the rear wheels in alternate forward and reverse motion; a steerable front roller is fitted. Fairly common. Length: 7·625in (19·3675cm).

3 Fire Service Car by an unidentified French maker, dating from around 1935-40. This was originally made as a novelty confectionary tin, its hinged roof forming a lid, and was intended to function as a toy when emptied; see also (11). Its tinplate body is pleasingly printed with such details as radiator grille, bonnet ventilators, a crest on the

door and a crew of firemen. The pressing incorporates a front bumper and close-fitting mud-guards and running-boards. A clockwork motor with a wire spring drives the rear wheels; note the permanently-fixed winder. It is fitted with pressed-tin wheels with printed details of "Dunlop" tyres. This is of limited availability, and in the case of such items toy collectors are likely to face stiff competition from collectors of tinplate containers — a rivalry that may well be reflected in the prices that are demanded! Length: 6·625in (16·8275cm).

4 "Ubilda" Fire Engine by Chad Valley, Great Britain; dating from around 1950. Chad Valley produced a number of vehicle construction kits in its "Ubilda" series both before and after World War II,

among them the tinplate fire engine which is shown here fully assembled. Nuts, bolts, axles, a clockwork motor and a spanner were supplied with the kit, and assembly of the sectional body and detachable fire escape on the pressed-tin chassis was quite simple. A separate key was provided for the clockwork motor, which drives the rear wheels. The radiator bears the printed number-plate "C.V. 10033". Limited. Length: 10·5in (26·67cm).

5 Fire Engine by C. Rossignol, Paris, France; dating from around 1940. Bearing the maker's "C.R." mark on the lower edge of its bonnet, this simple push-along toy is of lightweight tinplate, with a pressed chassis and printed cab and bonnet. It is fitted with a simple

revolving turntable ladder and has single-sided tinplate wheels. Limited. Length: 7·5in (19·05cm).

6 Turntable Fire Engine by an unidentified maker, probably of British or German manufacture; dating from around 1954. This forward-control vehicle is of lightweight tinplate construction; it has printed details and is equipped with two pressed-tin figures of seated firemen. A clockwork motor with a separate key (note the winding-shank towards the rear of the vehicle) drives the rear wheels. The nearside rear mudguard is missing. It is a limited item. Length: 10·00in (25·4cm).

7 Fire Engine by Jep (Jouets en Paris), France; dating from the 1930s. This two-seater fire engine with its pressed-tin firemen is a

rather pleasingly proportioned toy from a notable maker. It has printed details and is fitted with an elevating ladder. It has single-sided pressed-tin wheels, the rear pair driven by a clockwork motor with diecast cogs; note the rather over-sized permanently-fixed winder towards the rear of the chassis. Limited. Length: 7·625in (19·367cm).

8 "Breakdown Service" Lorry by an unidentified British maker; dating from around 1940. Note particularly the "Automobile Association" emblem on the cab doors; other printed details include radiator grille, bonnet ventilators, and spokes and "5 x 19 Balloon Tyres" on the two-piece pressed-tin wheels. The tinplate figure of the driver is just visible. A clockwork motor drives the rear wheels. The

manually-operated crane on the example shown is a replacement item. It is possible that this toy is the work of Wells Brimtoy. Limited. Length: 8·25in (20·955cm).

9 Ambulance by Gama, West Germany; dating from around 1955. This good-quality toy of heavy-gauge tinplate construction has a pressed body with an opening rear door and a bright-plated radiator grille and headlights. It is fitted with perforated-disc wheels with treaded black rubber tyres marked "10 x 35". The ambulance is fitted with a "push-and-go" mechanism that also produces a "siren" sound. A limited item. Length: 8·625in (21·9075cm).

10 Ambulance by Burnett Limited, Great Britain; dating from around 1940. This simple toy of lightweight

tinplate has a most attractive colour-printed finish; note that the mudguards and running-boards are edged with white, a common condition of real vehicles in the "blackout" conditions prevailing in Britain during the war years. This model is fitted with two-piece pressed-tin wheels, the rear pair driven by a clockwork motor with a permanently-fixed winder on the near side. This is a limited item. Length: 5·875in (14·9225cm).

11 Ambulance by an unidentified French maker; dating from around 1935-40. This is the same pressing as the Fire Service Car shown at (3); only the finish is different. Like (3), this ambulance has a hinged roof and was originally made as a novelty confectionary tin. Limited. Length: 6·625in (16·827cm).

1 Fire Engine by "K", Japan; dating from 1958-59. This toy is fully described at (7), *pages 32-33*, where it is shown with its packaging. Length: 13in (33·02cm).

2 Fire Engine by Arnold, West Germany; dating from around 1956. This is a simple and strongly-made push-along toy of tabbed-and-slotted tinplate construction. It has a white metal ladder with a gilt bell on either side, but all other details are printed. The metal wheels are fitted with heavy-treaded rubber tyres; the maker's name is printed on the metal whitewalls. The crank-handle at the left rear of the two-section ladder is used to extend it via a simple cord-and-pulley system. Length: 11in (27·94cm).

3 Fire Engine by Lincoln International, "Empire Made" (Hong Kong);

dating from around 1968. This small tinplate toy has bright metal front bumpers, radiator, bonnet ornament, cab steps and wind-screen frame. A yellow plastic spotlight is mounted on the left side of the bonnet and a yellow plastic hose-drum, complete with clear plastic hose, in the centre of the body. It was sold complete with plastic figure of a fireman (shown at rear). The rubber wheels, the front pair friction-driven, are fitted with metal discs. The two-section ladder swivels freely on a turntable mounting and can easily be extended and elevated manually. Length: 7·125in (18·097cm).

4 Fire Chief Car by Ichiro, Japan; dating from around 1959. Modelled on a Ford saloon, with "Ford" numberplates at front and rear,

this tinplate car has bright metal details that include the frames of the tinted plastic windows at front and rear. Like most vehicles shown on this spread, it bears appropriate printed badges, and in this case the legend "Fire Chief". It has a pressed-tin interior with printed details. A yellow plastic spotlight is mounted in a swivelling socket on the roof. The rubber wheels are fitted with metal discs; the rear pair are friction-driven, motion producing a siren sound. Length: 9·5in (24·13cm).

5 Fire Escape Truck by an unidentified West German maker; dating from around 1957. This large and robust push-along toy is made of heavy-gauge tinplate. It is a simple pressing, with a bright metal radiator and plastic headlights, but

little other detail. The six wheels are made of moulded plastic and are single-sided. The escape swivels freely on its turntable; when the catch visible at the front of the turntable is released, a simple spring-loaded mechanism elevates and extends the escape ladder. Length: 15in (38·1cm).

6 Super Fire King Ladder Trailer by SSS International, Japan; dating from 1960-61. This is an attractive and well-detailed tinplate toy. The cab has the usual bright metal details, including a divided frame for the clear plastic windscreen, and has a pressed and printed interior complete with steering wheel. Note the pressed-tin fuel tanks and, on the articulated trailer, the raised gilt "S.F.D." lettering and gilt platforms. The trailer also

features retractable pressed-tin stabilisers, a seat and wheel for simulated rear steering, and bright pressed-tin wheels that are used manually to raise and extend the ladder (via worm-gear) on its revolving turntable. The wheels of the vehicle are metal with heavy-treaded rubber tyres; friction drives the front wheels of the cab. Length: 17·75in (45·085cm).

7 Fire Command Car by "T.N." (Nomura Toys), Japan; dating from 1958-59. This large and impressive tinplate toy has a bright metal front bumper and metal mesh radiator; an inset metal "FD" emblem on the bonnet and an applied "Fire Dept. No.1" badge below its clear plastic windscreen; well-modelled, articulated tinplate figures of driver and passenger;

and a pressed-tin radio and jerrican at the rear. The wheels are rubber with metal discs; note the rear-mounted spare. Batteries housed in a base trap drive a two-wheeled turntable mounted towards the front of the base. The vehicle pursues an erratic course as the driver appears to steer; when it stops, intermittently, a buzzer sounds, the passenger raises his radio-telephone to his ear, and green plastic lights flash on either side of the radio set. Length: 11in (27·94cm).

8 Fire Engine by "K", Japan, dating from around 1958. This closely resembles the toy by the same maker at (1): some details of the colour printing vary, the ladder is of different construction and has no fireman at its upper end, but the

same pressing appears to have been used for the bodies of the two vehicles. Note that the lever operating the pop-up ladder is clearly seen in this photograph. Length: 13in (33·02cm).

9 Fire Department Car by unidentified Japanese maker; dating from around 1960. A fairly typical cheap tinplate toy, with most details printed and a pressed-out printed spotlight on the roof. The wheels are rubber with metal discs; the rear pair are friction-driven. The words "Made in Japan" are printed below the "F.D." badge on the boot. Length: 6·375in (16·19cm).

10 Fire Engine by "T.N." (Nomura Toys), Japan; dating from around 1961. This toy is of good-quality tinplate, with a wealth of printed detail and bumpers, radiator,

headlights and rear platform of bright metal. The tinplate firemen are attractively modelled, and the whole has a most pleasant "toy-like" quality. The rubber wheels are fitted with metal discs; the rear pair are friction-driven. As the vehicle moves, a siren noise is produced and the fireman mounted on the left of the cab (nearest camera) raises and lowers his articulated arm with its red flag. Length: 10·5in (26·67cm).

11 Fire Chief Car by an unidentified Japanese maker; dating from around 1960. This simple saloon car with brightly-printed details has bright metal bumpers, radiator and headlights. Its rubber wheels are fitted with metal discs and the rear pair are friction-driven. Length: 5·375in (13·6525cm).

1 T.V. Control Highway Patrol Car by an unidentified Japanese maker; dating from around 1959. Based on a Chevrolet Impala (note the applied "Chevrolet" lettering on the bonnet), with the "Highway Patrol" and "Police Department" lettering and colourfully-printed badges that are common to most of the toys on this spread, this tinplate car has a well-modelled radiator of bright metal, into which are set plastic-lensed headlights. It has tinted plastic windows at front and rear and a printed interior with a plastic steering wheel (left-hand drive). The red plastic warning light on the roof lights up when the car is in motion. The wheels are rubber, with well-modelled metal discs and printed hubcaps. It is powered by a battery housed in a base trap,

driving a bump-and-go turntable mounted towards the front of the base. The metal remote-control handset incorporates an on/off switch and a button that controls a siren sound. The "TV screen" on the handset lights up and, when not used for remote-control, may be clipped to the bracket on the car's boot. See also car at (2). Length: 14in (35·56cm).

2 Highway Patrol Car by an unidentified Japanese maker; dating from around 1959. This is in all respects save one—it has no remote-control facility—the same model as (1), and is again battery-powered with bump-and-go action. An on/off switch is situated towards the front of the base. Length: 14in (35·56cm).

3 Ford Highway Patrol Car by Ichiko,

Japan; dating from around 1958. This tinplate friction-driven car is fully described at (1), *pages 32-33*, where its packaging is shown. Length: 9·375in (23·81cm).

4 Highway Patrol Car by an unidentified Japanese maker; dating from around 1959. Bearing the usual printed lettering and badges, and with bright metal radiator, bumpers, trim strips and windscreen frames, this car has "Lincoln" numberplates at front and rear, windows of tinted plastic and has a printed interior with a plastic steering wheel (left-hand drive). A coloured plastic spotlight is mounted on the bonnet and the bright metal warning light on the roof has a red plastic lens. The wheels are rubber, with metal discs with printed whitewalls and

hubcaps. Friction drives the rear wheels: as the car moves, the warning light revolves and a siren noise is also produced. Length: 11·125in (28·257cm).

5 Remote-Control Police Car by Arnold, West Germany; dating from 1952-53. Only the plastic "Police" sign in a raised metal housing on its roof indicates that this solid toy of good-quality tinplate is a police vehicle. It has rather crude bright metal bumpers and other details; its plastic wheels, with bright metal hubcaps, are fitted with rubber whitewall tyres. The toy is powered by Arnold's usual hand-cranked remote-control system; fully described at (5), *pages 32-33*. Length: 10in (25·4cm).

6 Police Car by an unidentified Japanese maker; dating from

Above: *Rear detail of [4]. When the screw is released with the special key and the catch set to "Open", the door opens and an alarm bell rings.*

around 1958. This simple Ford-type saloon, with bright metal and printed details, bears the rear numberplate "102507". Note the coiled-wire aerial with a red plastic knob. The wheels—the rear pair friction-driven, with siren sound—are rubber with metal discs. Length: 5·375in (13·65cm).

7 Police Car by an unidentified maker (it is stamped "Empire Made";presumably Hong Kong); dating from c1958. This rather crudely-pressed tinplate toy has a plastic "Police Car" plaque in a raised metal frame on the roof and has quite extensive bright metal details, including windscreen frames. The wing-mounted siren and radio aerial are plastic. The rubber wheels, the rear pair friction-driven with siren sound,

are fitted with bright metal discs. Length: 6in (15·24cm).

8 Patrol Auto-Tricycle by T.N. (Nomura Toys); dating from 1958-59. This well-made tinplate toy has an ingenious action: batteries housed in the base drive a rear wheel to give a figure-eight course, while the driver appears to steer. The action is stop-start: when it stops, the driver's whistle sounds; when it moves the headlight operates. It has treaded rubber wheels with printed metal discs. Length: 9·75in (24·765cm).

9 Armoured Car Savings Bank by "H", Japan; dating from c1958. This attractively-printed novelty toy has bright metal front and rear bumpers and headlights. It has a divided windscreen of clear plastic and a printed cab with a plastic

steering wheel (left-hand drive). The rubber wheels, the front pair friction-driven, are fitted with metal discs. Note the money slot at top rear; and see *Inset* for more detail. Length: 10in (25·4cm).

10 Mystery Police Car by T.N. (Nomura Toys), Japan; dating from c1960. This is an attractive tinplate toy with bright metal details that include applied "Police" lettering and a siren, with a pressed-tin radio set mounted at the rear. It has rubber wheels with metal discs. Batteries power a two-wheeled bump-and-go turntable mounted between the front wheels. The articulated driver is linked to the wheels so that he appears to steer the car. As it moves, a siren sound is made and the blue light flashes. Length: 10in (25·4cm).

11 Bump-'n-Go F.B.I.Car by "K.O.", Japan; dating from c1959. Its wheels are printed pressed-tin. A friction flywheel, activated by a crank-handle on the base, drives the wheels of a front-mounted bump-and-go turntable. As the car moves, the pressed-tin driver traverses his plastic machine gun and a "firing" noise is made. Length: 6·5in (16·51cm).

12 Police Car by "K.O.", Japan; dating from c1960. It has a pair of pressed-tin wheels at the rear: at the front are two rubber wheels of a bump-and-go turntable, powered by batteries. As the car moves, the warning light on the bonnet flashes and the articulated pressed-tin driver cranks his siren, with an appropriate sound. Length: 7·75in (19·685cm).

1 Power Shovel by SSS Quality Toys, Japan (presumably an offshoot of SSS International); dating from 1959-60. This robust tinplate toy is made in two parts: a circular turret-mount on the base of the mechanical shovel's cab slots into a half-moon recess on the body of the six-wheeled push-along truck, permitting the shovel to swivel freely. Note the steps to the cab on the truck, and the effective pressed details of the cab roof and exhaust stacks. The truck has yellow-and-black printed bumpers. Its steerable front wheels are rubber with metal discs; the rear wheels (both pairs double) are metal, fitted with treaded rubber tyres and featuring simple suspension brackets. To operate the power shovel, the long lever on the side of the cab is pulled back to "cock" a clockwork mechanism: when the control button on the top of the cab is depressed, the shovel performs repeated scooping, raising and dumping actions. Lengths: (truck chassis) 12·75in (32·385cm); (with shovel extended) 16in (40·64cm).

2 Automatic Dock Crane by Biller, West Germany; dating from c1958. This well-made and colourful tinplate toy, with railway lines and a turntable printed on top of its base and transport scenes around the sides, is clockwork-powered; note permanent winder at end of base. The wooden-handled lever to the right of the winder is the on/off control; the lever to the left controls the rotation of the crane and the raising and lowering of its jib. The plunger below the left-hand lever activates a wire that runs through a spring-loaded suspension arm to open or close the crane's bucket. Length of base: 8·5in (21·59cm); height of crane: 7in (17·78cm).

3 Mechanical Digger by Gama, West Germany; serial number 282, dating from c1956. This fine mechanical toy is of heavy-gauge tinplate, with a plastic spotlight, clear plastic windows, and white rubber crawler tracks on metal wheels. Its clockwork mechanism is wound via the long yellow crank on its side. The on/off lever and the levers controlling the powered raising and lowering of the bucket, via pulleys and chains, are at the rear of the cab. The knurled knob (on the left in photograph) is for manual traverse of the jib; the lever on the right manually adjusts the jib's elevation. Length (including jib): 16·75in (42·545cm).

4 Mechanical Digger by Gama, West Germany; serial number 2808, dating from c1957. This toy has a tough plastic cab but is otherwise of good-quality tinplate. Batteries housed in a recess in the base power the wheels, with white rubber crawler tracks, and light up the roof-mounted, plastic-housed spots when the digger is in motion. Otherwise, all operations are manual: a lever on the right (in photograph) controls the jib's elevation; a crank handle on the left raises, lowers, opens or closes the bucket. Length (jib included): 16in (40·64cm).

5 Electric Motor Crane by MFZ, West Germany; dating from c 1955. The rims of the roof-mounted spotlights

are plastic and the crawler tracks are white rubber, otherwise this fairly simply-made toy is tinplate throughout. Batteries housed in the base power the wheels, spotlights and, via a lever mounted at the back of the cab, the pulley-and-chain mechanism of the bucket. The larger lever at the rear of the cab is for manual elevation or depression of the jib. Length (including jib): 14in (35·56cm).

6 Magic Action Bulldozer by T.N. (Nomura Toys), Japan; dating from c1958. In this fine toy, note the wealth of printed detail and, in particular, the truly remarkable press-work that has gone into the well-articulated, detachable figure of the driver. Batteries housed in a trap on the base drive a bump-and-go action turntable mounted

towards the front of the base. The on/off switch is visible near the driver's foot. When the vehicle moves, the black rubber crawler tracks revolve; the coloured plastic lights on the printed tin engine flash beneath the clear plastic bonnet; and cranks from the turntable move the levers "held" by the driver so that he appears to steer the vehicle. An engine noise is also produced. Length: 9·625in (24·45cm).

7 Mechanical Shovel and Trailer by Gescha, West Germany; dating from c1953. The maker's name and the number "B-720" are printed along the bottom of the shovel unit's white metal radiator. The shovel unit has a plastic exhaust stack and steering wheel and is fitted with white rubber crawler tracks; the figure of the driver

is composition, otherwise the toy is of fairly good-quality tinplate throughout. It is unpowered: a crank mounted on the side away from the camera is used to lower the shovel and to raise it through an angle of more than 90°, so that sand or gravel may be picked up from in front and dumped to the rear — perhaps into the waiting trailer, which engages with a hook on the shovel's rear; the trailer has a tipping mechanism operated by a lever mounted on the side away from the camera, and a hinged tail-gate. The trailer's wheels are metal, with treaded rubber tyres. Lengths: (shovel unit, with shovel lowered) 8·375in (21·27cm); (trailer, with draw-bar) 11in (27·94cm).

8 Remote-Controlled Bulldozer by Arnold, West Germany; dating

from 1956-57. This high-quality toy was marketed both assembled (as shown) and in construction kit form. The major parts are tinplate with printed details. The drive wheels are plastic, with wooden idler wheels for the black rubber crawler tracks; the figure of the driver is plastic, as is his seat. The lever to the driver's right is for the manual raising or lowering of the blade (which has the maker's name printed across it), which is locked into place by small protrusions that fit into grooves on the sides of the radiator. The toy is powered by Arnold's own ingenious mechanism — described at length at (5), *pages 32-33* — via a cored cable from the hand-cranked control set, with a plunger that steers the vehicle. Length overall: 11·375in (28·89).

1-4 Six-wheeled Wagon by Dinky Toys, Great Britain; Dinky Toys Reference Number (DT No) 25s. First issued in 1938, this model is near-identical with the Three-Ton Transport Wagon (DT No 151b) issued as part of the Royal Tank Corps Medium Tank Set in February 1938. The only differences are that the Six-Wheeled Wagon appeared in non-military finishes—reddish-brown, as at (1) and (2), being the most common—usually with its detachable tinplate canopy in grey, and that it was without the tinplate insert that provided bench seats (with holes pierced for peg-in passengers) in the rear of the military version. This model has a cast-in steering wheel, is fitted with a spare wheel on the driver's door and a towing-hook at the rear, and

has a tinplate base plate stamped with the maker's name. The model remained in production until 1940 and was reissued after World War II, in 1948-48. The major difference between pre- and post-War versions is that the former always has a hole pierced in the front seat for the peg-in figure of a driver (which had to be purchased separately), whereas the latter usually (but not invariably) does not have this feature. Of the examples shown, (1) is pre-War, with hole for driver and white rubber tyres; (2) and (3) have black rubber tyres, but also pierced front seats; (4), shown with canopy removed, is a post-War example with an un-pierced front seat. Pre-War versions are limited; post-War versions fairly common. Length: 3·976in (101mm).

5-7 Petrol Tank Wagon; DT No 25d. This model appeared in a variety of forms over a long period, with different transfers. The various versions not shown here may be briefly summarised as follows: (i) Petrol Tank Wagon without transfers, issued 1934-38, Type 1 (open chassis, tinplate radiator without headlights), 4·252in (108mm); (ii) "Shell B.P.", 1936-38, other details as (i); (iii) "Petrol", 1938-40, Type 2 (open chassis, diecast radiator with headlights), 4·094in (104mm); (iv) "Shell B.P.", 1939-40, Type 2, 4·21in (107mm); (v) "Texaco", 1936-40, other details as (iv); (vi) "Power", 1939-40, other details as (iv); (vii) "Esso", 1939-40, other details as (iv); (viii) "Mobiloil" (red body), 1939-40, other details as (iv); (ix)

"Castrol", 1939-40, other details as (iv); (x) "Power" (gold logo), 1939-40, other details as (iv); (xi) "Redline-Glico", 1939-40, other details as (iv); (xii) "Shell B.P." (gold logo), 1939-40, other details as (iv); (xiii) "Texaco" (white logo), 1939-40, other details as (iv); (xiv) "Mobiloil" (orange body), 1939-40, other details as (iv); (xv) "Pool", 1940-41, other details as (iv). The versions shown here are those produced post-War: at (5) and (6), "Petrol", issued in 1946-47, Type 3 (plain chassis, diecast radiator with headlights), 4·094in (104mm); at (7), "Petrol", issued in 1947-50, Type 4 (moulded chassis, bumper fitted, diecast radiator with headlights), 4·3125in (110mm). The post-War examples shown here are of limited availability; pre-War

items now verge on scarcity.

8-11 Market Gardener's Van; DT No 25f. All four versions of this model are shown here. At (8), as issued between April 1934 and 1938; Type 1, with a tinplate radiator without headlights and an open chassis; note also the white rubber tyres. At (9), as issued 1938-40; Type 2, with a diecast radiator with headlights and an open chassis. At (10), as issued 1947-50; Type 4, with diecast radiator with headlights and bumper and a moulded chassis. At (11), as issued 1946-47; Type 3, with a diecast radiator with headlights and a plain chassis. All versions are fitted with a towing-hook. The pre-War versions are limited; post-War items are fairly common. Lengths: (Type 1) 4·21in (107mm); (Types 2 and 3)

4·134in (105mm); (Type 4) 4·3125in (110mm).

12-13 Covered Wagon; DT No 25b. The two final issues of this model are shown here: at (12), as issued 1946-47, Type 3; at (13), as issued 1947-50, Type 4. The model first appeared in April 1934 and before World War II was issued in a Type 1 version without advertising transfers, and in three Type 2 versions, with advertising for "Hornby Trains", "Meccano" and "Carter Paterson" respectively. The versions with advertising are scarce; the pre-War model without advertising is limited; post-War versions are fairly common. Lengths: (Type 3 wagon) 4·134in (105mm); (Type 4 wagon) 4·3125in (110mm).

14-15 Tipping Wagon; DT No 25e. This

model first appeared in April 1934 and was produced in Type 1 and Type 2 versions before World War II. The versions shown here are: (14) as issued 1947-50; Type 4; (15) as issued 1946-47, Type 3. All versions have a manual tipping action and all are fitted with a towing-hook at the rear. Pre-War versions are limited; post-War models are fairly common. Lengths: (Type 3) 4·134in (105mm); (Type 4) 4·3125in (110mm).

16-18 Flat Truck; DT No 25c. This model was announced in April 1934, but may not have been made in a Type 1 form. The examples shown here are: (16), as issued 1938-40, Type 2; (17), as issued 1947-50, Type 4; (18), as issued 1946-47, Type 3. The model at (18) is shown towing the

Four-Wheeled Trailer, DT No 25g, which first appeared in 1935, was made until 1940 (tinplate tow-bar), 1947 on (wire tow-bar), renumbered 429 in 1954 and was produced until 1963. Common. Pre-War trucks are limited; post-War versions fairly common. Lengths: (Types 2 and 3) 4·134in (105mm); (Type 4) 4·3125in (110mm).

19-20 Wagon; DT No 25a. This model was announced in April 1934 but, as in the case of the Flat Truck (16-18), it is possible that no Type 1 version was made. A Type 2 version was available in 1938-40. Both the examples shown here are Type 3, available 1946-47; a Type 4 was made in 1947-50. Pre-War versions are limited; post-War versions are fairly common. Length: (Type 3) 4·134in (105mm).

1-4 Mechanical Horse and Open Wagon by Dinky Toys, Great Britain; Dinky Toys Reference Number (DT No) 33w. This model, issued in October 1947, used the castings for two pre-World War II models: the three-wheeled Mechanical Horse (DT No 33a, in production 1935-40) and the two-wheeled Open Truck Trailer (DT No 33c, in production 1935-40). The original version, appearing in brown, as at (1) and (4), olive green (3) and other colours, had a tinplate base plate stamped with the maker's name. In 1953 it was reissued, now all diecast and again with the maker's name: the commonest colour finish for the later version is a blue horse and cream trailer, as shown at (2). The model was renumbered 415 in 1954 and

remained in production until 1959. It is fairly common; the earlier version may be harder to find. Lengths: (horse) 2·48in (63mm); (trailer) 2·441in (62mm); (overall length of model when assembled) 4·016in (102mm).

5 Austin Wagon; DT No 412, first issued in June 1950, when it was numbered 30j, renumbered 412 in 1954, and in production until 1960. It appeared in blue, as shown, brown and maroon (and possibly other colours). It is fitted with a towing-hook and has a tinplate base plate stamped with the maker's name, "30J" (missing from later examples) and "Austin". It is still a fairly common model. Length: 4.094 (104mm).

6 Austin Covered Wagon; DT No 413. Issued in September 1950, when it

was numbered 30s, this model used the same casting as (5), with the addition of a tinplate canopy. It was renumbered 413 in 1954 and remained in production until 1960. Appearing in maroon-and-fawn, as shown, and other colour combinations, it is fitted with a towing-hook and has a tinplate base plate stamped with the maker's name, "30S" and "Austin". It is fairly common. The model was also issued for sale in the USA, in US Army olive-green finish, at first numbered 30sm and then 625. Length: 4·094in (104mm).

7 Bedford Articulated Flat Truck; Dinky Dublo No 072, issued in June 1959 and in production until 1964. Dinky Dublo models, in "00" scale for use with Hornby Dublo toy train layouts, were introduced in

December 1957. The series was not very successful, perhaps because Lesney's "Matchbox" range dominated the British market for small diecast toys, and only 20 models (including railway staff and other figures, cars and commercial vehicles) were issued in 1957-70. All Dinky Dublo vehicles have solid wheels of grey or black plastic; some, like this example, have clear plastic windows. All were made in only one finish; in this case, yellow/orange-and-red. This is a fairly common item. Length: 4·567in (116mm).

8 Bedford Flat Truck; Dinky Dublo No 066, issued in December 1957 and in production until 1960. It has no windows; see note at (7). This will be quite easy to find. Length: 4·567in (116mm).

9-10 Fordson Thames Flat Truck; DT No 30r, issued in February 1951, renumbered 422 in March 1954, and in production until 1960. Appearing only in red or green, it is fitted with a towing-hook. The earlier version has a tinplate base plate stamped with the maker's name and "Fordson"; on the post-renumbering version, which was marketed as "Thames Flat Truck", the number "422" also appears. Some later versions may have clear plastic windows: these are harder to find than other versions, which are fairly common. The example at (9) is towing the Four-Wheeled Trailer (DT No 25g); see note at (16-18), *pages 62-63.* Length: 4·409in (112mm).

11 Rear Tipping Wagon; DT No 30m, issued in August 1950, renumbered 414 in 1954, and in production until 1964. Before renumbering, this was made in orange; after renumbering, when it was marketed as "Dodge Rear Tipping Wagon", in grey-and-blue, as shown, and green-and-orange. A crank-handle on the left side raises the tipping mechanism; it has a hinged tailboard and a tinplate base plate. It is a fairly common item. Length: 3·898in (99mm).

12-13 Farm Produce Wagon; DT No 30n, issued in May 1950, renumbered 343 in 1954, and in production until 1964. Using the same Dodge casting as (11), this model appeared in green-and-yellow (12) or, less commonly, red-and-blue (13). It is fitted with a towing-hook but, according to authoritative sources, should *not*

feature the tipping action shown at (12). It is a fairly common item. Length: 4·21in (107mm).

14-15 Forward Control Lorry; DT No 25r, issued in May 1948, renumbered 420 in October 1954, and in production, latterly as "Leyland Forward Control Lorry", until 1961. This model appeared in green (14), cream (15), red or grey; it is fitted with a towing-hook. Fairly common. Length: 4·21in (107mm).

16-18 Bedford Breakdown Van; DT No 30e, issued in August 1935 and in production until 1940, and reissued in 1946-48. All versions are one-piece castings fitted with a solid cast searchlight and crane, the latter with a wire hook. Pre-War versions have a rear window in the cab; on post-War versions, this is filled in. Of the examples shown

here, (16) and (17) are post-War versions; (18) is a pre-War model, distinguished not only by the rear window (which cannot be seen in the photograph), but also by its black-painted front and rear wings and white rubber tyres. The pre-War model is limited, verging on scarce; post-War versions are fairly common. Length: 3·622in (92mm).

19-20 Motor Truck; DT No 22c, first issued in May 1935. This was in production until 1940 and was reissued in 1946-50. As at (16-18), pre-War models have a rear window in the cab and post-War models have not. Of the examples shown here, (19) is pre-War — note the white rubber tyres; (20) is post-War. The pre-War version is limited; the post-War version is fairly common. Length: 3·307in (84mm).

1-2 Renault Covered Wagon (*Camion 7-T Renault*) by L.E., France; dating from the 1950s. It is interesting to compare this model by a lesser-known maker with the similar models made by Dinky Toys, France, around the same time. In a smaller scale than the Dinky models shown here, but quite well detailed, this lorry is fitted with a tinplate canopy. The example at (1) has a wire towing-hook; the lorry at (2) possibly a later production version, has a tinplate towing-hook. Limited. Lengths: (1) 4·134in (105mm); (2) 4·3125in (110mm).

3 Renault Tipping Truck by CIJ, France; dating from the 1950s. The cab and chassis are very solidly cast; the tipping rear body (activated by a lever on the side

away from the camera) is of tinplate. Limited. Length: 4·134in (105mm).

4 Two-Wheeled Covered Trailer (*Remorque à deux roues bâchée*) by Dinky Toys, France; French Dinky Toys Reference Number (FDT No) 25T, issued in June 1949 and in production until March 1955. This was based on the Two-Wheeled Trailer, FDT No 25S, produced in 1948-52, with the addition of a tinplate canopy. The tow-bar is soldered to the front and a towing-hook is fitted at the rear. The model appeared in a number of colour combinations, at first (1949 only) with metal wheels, and then, as shown, with cast wheels fitted with smooth black rubber tyres. Like most French Dinky Toys, its availability in Great Britain is limited. Length: 2·9375in (75mm).

5 Four-Wheeled Covered Trailer by L.E., France; dating from the 1950s. It has a bright tinplate tow-bar, a swivelling front axle and a tinplate canopy. A limited item. Length: 3·346in (85mm).

6 Ford Tipping Wagon (*Ford Benne basculante*); FDT No 25M, issued in 1950 and in production until 1955. The tipping action of the rear body is activated by a crank-handle on the left side of the chassis. A hinged tailboard is fitted. Earlier versions have black wheels, as shown; later ones (1954-55) have green wheels. See (15) for a similar model, with the same reference number, with a Studebaker cab. Limited. Length: 3·70in (94mm).

7 Ford Tanker Wagon "Esso" (*Ford Camion Citerne "Esso"*); FDT No 25U, issued in 1950 and in

production until 1952. This model was originally intended to have a towing-hook and a spare wheel, and early versions will be found with the tinplate base cut away to accommodate a moulded support for these features, which were never fitted. The red finish was standard, but later versions (1952) have smaller "Esso" decals on the sides and rear. A limited item. Length: 4·134in (105mm).

8 Ford Cattle Wagon (*Ford Bétaillère*); FDT No 25A, issued in 1950 and in production until 1952. It is fitted with a spare wheel and a tinplate towing-hook. As well as the finish shown, it appeared in metallic-light-blue with yellow wheels; a version with a yellow cab and red rear body and wheels is rare. Limited. Length: 3·70in (94mm).

9 Ford Milk Wagon (*Ford laitier*); FDT No 250, issued in 1950 and in production until 1954. This model has ten moulded milk churns on the lower sides and ten removable churns that are housed in the upper body. It is fitted with a spare wheel and a towing-hook. The "Nestle" legend may be found as either a stamp or a decal. Limited. Length: 3·70in (94mm).

10 Ford Covered Wagon "Grands Moulins De Paris" (*Ford Camion Bache "Grands Moulins De Paris"*); FDT No 25JV, issued in 1951 and in production until 1953. The example shown is of the second type (1953), finished in grey with a black canopy (note that part of the decal is missing from this example) and red wheels; an early version with the body finished

in green is much rarer. Limited. Length: 4·016in (102mm).

11 Ford Recovery Wagon with Crane (*Ford Dépannage avec Grue*); FDT No 25R, issued in April 1954 and in production until March 1955. Fitted wth a tinplate crane and towing-hook, this model has "Dinky Service" stamped on its tailboard. A late production version, without the advertisement and with chromed wheels fitted with white tyres, is rare. A limited model. Length: 4·606in (117mm).

12 Ford Refuse Wagon (*Ford benne à ordures*); FDT No 25V, issued in October 1950 and in production until 1955. The rear body, tipping by means of rack mechanism, is of pressed tinplate, with two sliding covers and a hinged rear flap. Limited. Length: 3·74in (95mm).

13 Ford Beverage Truck (*Ford Plateau Brasseur*); FDT No 25H, issued in 1949 and in production until 1960. This model appeared in a wide variety of colour finishes; early versions have metal wheels, but later ones have rubber tyres. Limited. Length: 4·016in (102mm).

14 Studebaker Market Gardener's Van (*Studebaker Maraicher*); FDT No 25K, issued in 1949 and in production until 1952. This model, which appeared in various two-tone finishes, is fitted with a spare wheel. Limited. Length: 4·134in (105mm).

15 Studebaker Tipping Wagon (*Studebaker Benne basculante*); FDT No 25M, issued in May 1949 and in production until April 1954. As (6), with Studebaker cab. Limited Length: 4·134in (105mm).

16 Studebaker Covered Van

(*Studebaker Camionnette bâchée*); FDT No 25Q, issued in June 1949 and in production until 1952. Fitted with a tinplate canopy, this model appeared always in two-tone finish. Length: 4·134in (105mm).

17 Studebaker Milk Wagon (*Studebaker Laitier*); FDT No 250, issued in April 1949 and in production until April 1954. As (9), with Studebaker cab. Limited. Length: 4·134in (105mm).

18 Studebaker Breakdown Van with Crane (*Studebaker Camionnette de dépannage avec grue*); FDT No 25R, issued in May 1949 and in production until April 1954. Examples made in 1949 only are to be found with metal wheels and without the "Dinky Service" stamp along the sides of the vehicle. Limited. Length: 4·724in (120mm).

1 Foden 14-Ton Tanker, "Regent", by Dinky Toys, Great Britain; Dinky Toys Reference Number (DT No) 942, issued in June 1955 and in production until 1957. This most attractive model in the Dinky Supertoys range appeared only in the red-white-and-blue finish seen here, with "Regent" in gold. It has an eight-wheeled chassis and is fitted with the second-type Foden radiator; see (10) for an example of the first-type radiator. It has detachable treaded rubber tyres, with a spare wheel fitted beneath the body. The tinplate base plate is stamped with the maker's name and "Foden". Limited; becoming scarce. Length: 7·402in (188mm).

2 Foden Flat Truck with Chains; DT No 505. This Supertoys model was issued in September 1955, and

remained in production until 1964. It appeared throughout its life in green, as shown, and was also made in maroon in 1952-54. The eight-wheeled chassis is the same as that of (1); again, it has a second-type Foden radiator, a spare wheel beneath its body, and a tinplate base plate stamped with the maker's name and "Foden". It is a limited item. Length: 7·402in (188mm).

3 Racehorse Transport; DT No 979. This Supertoys model was issued in October 1961 and was in production until 1964. It appeared only in pale-grey-and-yellow finish, with "Racehorse Transport" and a horse's-head logo above the cab and "Newmarket Racehorse Transport Service Ltd" and the same logo on the sides. It is fitted with opening side and rear doors

that hinge down to form ramps. Its diecast base bears the maker's name and "Horsebox". It was sold complete with two plastic horses (not shown). A limited item. Length: 6·889in (175mm).

4 Horse Box; DT No 581, issued in April 1953, renumbered 981 in January 1955, and in production until 1960. Appearing only in maroon, this model bears "British Railways" decals above the cab and on the sides towards the rear, and (not visible in the photograph because the ramp is lowered) the decals "Express/Horse Box/Hire Service" on the sides towards the front. It was issued in the USA without "British Railways" decals. The side and rear ramps are hinged and it has a diecast base bearing the maker's name and

"Horse box". A limited item. Length: 6·889in (175mm).

5 4000-Gallon Tanker, "Shell BP"; DT No 944, issued in July 1963 and in production until 1970. This Supertoys model on the eight-wheeled Leyland Octopus chassis has "Shell" and "BP" on the sides of its plastic tank. It appeared only in yellow-and-white. Clear plastic windows are fitted and there is a towing-hook at the rear. Its tinplate base bears the maker's name and "Leyland Octopus". A limited item. Length: 7·559in (192mm).

6 Leyland Octopus Tanker, "Esso"; DT No 943, issued in March 1958 and in production until 1964. This Supertoys model appeared only in red, with "Esso Petroleum Company Ltd" decals on sides and back. Note that the diecast tank incorporates

a ladder and catwalk. Its tinplate base plate bears the maker's name and "Leyland Octopus". Limited. Length: 7·559in (192mm).

7 Leyland Octopus Wagon; DT No 934, issued in April 1956 and in production until 1964. This Supertoys model appeared in various two-tone finishes; see also (9). Using the same chassis as (5) and (6), it is fitted with spare wheel and hook. Limited. Length: 7·638in (194mm).

8 Leyland Octopus Flat Truck with Chains; DT No 935, issued in 1964 and in production until 1966. Using the same chassis as (5-7), this appeared in various two-tone finishes. It is a limited item. Length: 7·559in (192mm).

9 Leyland Octopus Wagon; a colour variation of the model shown at (7).

10 Foden Diesel Eight-Wheel Wagon; DT No 501, issued in 1947 and in production until 1952. This was one of the first Dinky Supertoys— see also (11) and (12); it is a one-piece casting with the first-type Foden radiator. It appeared in various two-tone finishes. On the earliest models, no towing-hook is fitted at the rear of the eight-wheeled chassis (with spare wheel fitted beneath). It has a tinplate base plate stamped with the maker's name and "Foden". The model was reissued with the second-type Foden radiator in 1952, was renumbered 901 in 1954, and remained in production until 1957. All versions are of limited availability. Length: 7·402in (188mm).

11 Foden Flat Truck; DT No 502, issued in October 1947 and in production until 1952, when it was reissued as DT No 902 with the second-type Foden radiator, remaining in production until 1960. It is always found with a towing-hook. A limited item; but more easily found than (10). Length: 7·402in (188mm).

12 Foden Flat Truck with Tailboard; DT No 503, issued in October 1947, reissued with the second-type radiator in 1952, renumbered 903 in 1954, and remaining in production until 1960. Limited; as (10). Length: 7·402in (188mm).

13 Foden Flat Truck with Chains; DT No 505, issued in January 1952 and in production in its original form in 1952 only. In September 1952 it was reissued with the second-type radiator; it was renumbered 905 in 1954 and remained in production until 1964.

It is limited; the later versions may prove to be harder to find. Length: 7·402in (188mm).

14 Foden 14-Ton Tanker; DT No 504. As seen here, with the first-type radiator, this Supertoys model was first issued in December 1948, in two-tone blue or red-and-fawn finish, remaining available until 1952. It was made with the second-type radiator, in two-tone blue finish only, in 1953-54; in 1953 there appeared also a version with second-type radiator, in red finish, with "Mobilgas" decals on its tinplate tank. The "Mobilgas" version was renumbered 941 in 1954 and remained in production until 1957. The first two versions of this model are of limited availability; the "Mobilgas" version is scarce. Length: 7·402in (188mm).

1 B.B.C. TV Mobile Control Room by Dinky Toys, Great Britain; Dinky Toys Reference Number (DT No) 967, issued in July 1959 and in production until 1964. This Dinky Supertoys model is fitted with clear plastic windows and bears "B.B.C. Television Service" and coats-of-arms decals. It has a tinplate base plate stamped with the maker's name, "967" and "TV mobile control room". A limited item. Length: 5·866in (149mm).
2 B.B.C. TV Extending Mast Vehicle; DT No 969, issued in October 1959 and in production until 1964. The metal mast is extended and elevated by a crank-handle; it has a rotating dish aerial at its top. The vehicle has clear plastic windows and bears B.B.C. coats-of-arms decals. Limited. Length: 6·496in (165mm).

3 B.B.C. TV Roving Eye Vehicle; DT No 968, issued in May 1959 and in production until 1964. This model was the first of the three "B.B.C. TV" Supertoys to be issued, and was the first large commercial vehicle by Dinky Toys to feature plastic windows. Both the mast and the figure of the cameraman are rotatable. A limited item. Length: 4·3125in (110mm).
4 A.B.C. TV Transmitter Van; DT No 988, issued in May 1962 and in production until 1968. This Supertoys models, with an "A.B.C.-TV" decal above the cab and a logo on the sides, has a revolving dish aerial on its roof. Its tinplate base plate is stamped with the maker's name and "Transmitter van". A limited item. Length: 4·449in (113mm).
5 A.B.C. TV Control Room; DT No

987, issued in July 1962 and in production until 1969. Completing the Supertoys "A.B.C.-TV" set, this bears the same decals as (4), plus "A.B.C. Television Service" along the upper sides. It was sold complete with the separate figures of a cameraman and camera (not shown), with plastic cables running from the camera to a "power panel" in the van's lower left side. It has a tinplate base plate stamped with the maker's name and "TV Mobile control room". A limited item. Length: 5·945in (151mm).
6-7 A.E.C. Tanker; DT No 591, issued in September 1952, renumbered 991 in January 1955, and in production until 1958. It appeared only in red-and-yellow finish. The earlier version shown at (6) has a "Shell Chemicals Limited" transfer;

the version at (7) dates from post-1955, when this became "Shell Chemicals". A transfer at the rear, indicating a 20mph speed restriction, was dropped in 1957. Both versions of the model are limited. Length: 5·945in (151mm).
8 Guy Van, "Ever Ready/Batteries for life!"; DT No 918, issued in December 1955 and in production until 1958. Like (9) and (10), this Supertoys model is fitted with the second-type Guy front and has opening rear doors, a spare wheel fitted beneath it, and a tinplate base plate stamped with the maker's name and "Guy". It is a limited item: verging on scarce. Length: 5·276in (134mm).
9 Guy Van, "Spratts/Spratt's Bonio, Ovals & Dog Cakes"; DT No 514, issued in July 1953, renumbered

917 in 1954, and in production until 1956. A scarce model. Length: 5·276in (134mm).

10 Guy Van, "Slumberland/Spring Interior/Mattresses" (with crest); DT No 514, issued in December 1949 and in production until 1952. Note that the number is the same as that used for (9). A limited item. Length: 5·276in (134mm).

11 Guy 4-Ton Lorry; DT No 911. This Supertoys model, with a Warrior-type Guy front, was issued in January 1954 as a renumbered version of DT No 511; see (20-21). It was renumbered 431 in 1956 and remained in production until 1964. Limited. Length: 5·197in (132mm).

12-13 Bedford Articulated Lorry; DT No 521, issued in April 1948, renumbered 921 in 1954, again renumbered 409 in 1956, and in

production until 1963. The colour finishes of the examples shown here are those most commonly found on this Supertoys model. It has a spare wheel fitted behind the cab and is equipped with a towing-hook. A common item. Length: (overall): 6·535in (166mm).

14/16-17 Bedford End Tipper; DT No 25m, issued in March 1948, renumbered 410 in 1954, and in production until 1963. A crank-handle on the left side of the body works via a worm-gear to tip the rear of the lorry, which has a hinged tailboard. The model originally appeared in orange (14), green (16), red-and-cream (17) and other colours. After renumbering, it appeared in brown-and-yellow and blue-and-yellow in 1955-63, and in red-and-cream, with the

addition of clear plastic windows, in 1962-63. Fairly common. Length: 3·858in (98mm).

15 Bedford Truck; DT No 25w, issued in February 1949, renumbered 411 in 1954, and in production until 1960. It appeared only in green finish, as seen here, and is fitted with a towing-hook. Its tinplate base plate is stamped with the maker's name and "Bedford". This is a fairly common item. Length: 4·094in (104mm).

16-17 Bedford End Tipper; see (14).

18 Guy Flat Truck with Tailboard; DT No 513, issued in October 1947, renumbered 913 in 1954, again renumbered 433 in 1956, and in production until 1958. This Super-toys model was originally made with first-type front and was fitted with the second-type front after

1954. All versions are limited. Length: 5·197in (132mm).

19 Guy Flat Truck; DT No 512, issued in October 1947, renumbered 912 in 1954, again renumbered 432 in 1956, and in production until 1958. All other details are as (18). Limited. Length: 5·197in (132mm).

20-21 Guy 4-Ton Lorry; DT No 511, issued in October 1947, re-numbered 911—see (11)—in 1954, again renumbered 431 in 1956, and in production until 1964. These examples have the first-type front. A limited item. Length: 5·197in (132mm).

22-23 Big Bedford Lorry; DT No 522, issued in October 1952, re-numbered 922 in 1954, again renumbered 408 in 1956, and in production until 1963. Limited. Length: 5·748in (146mm).

1 Tractor-Trailer, "McLean", by Dinky Toys, Great Britain; Dinky Toys Reference Number (DT No) 948, issued in April 1961 and in production until 1967. Appearing only in red-and-grey, with "McLean, Winston Salem" decals on the tractor and "McLean Trucking Company" on the trailer, this Dinky Supertoys model is fitted with opening rear doors. Limited. Lengths: (tractor) 4·291in (109mm); (trailer) 8·898 (226mm); (overall) 11·417in (290mm).

2 Pullmore Car Transporter with Ramp; DT No 582, issued in May 1953, renumbered 982 in 1954, and in production until 1964. This Supertoys model has "Dinky Toys Delivery Service" rubber-stamped on the trailer's lower deck. The model can accommodate four

Dinky cars and is equipped with a tinplate ramp, seen here in the unloading position. The tailgate of the lower deck hinges down to form a further ramp. The cab is the familiar Dinky Bedford type, which underwent a number of casting changes during the life of this model. Examples made before c1959 will be found without treaded Supertoys-type tyres. In later examples, the cab will have clear plastic windows. The model shown here, like the variant at (4), is of the earlier type. A variety of colour finishes are to be found, but the ramp will always be in light blue. Limited. Length overall: 9·843in (250mm).

3 A.E.C. Hoynor Car Transporter; DT No 974, issued in 1968 and in production until 1975. This model uses the same cab as the A.E.C.

with Flat Trailer (DT No 915, 1973-75). It has "SC" (Silcock & Colling Ltd) decals on the doors and is fitted with a hinged rear ramp and an adjustable-angle top deck. Its availability is now limited. Length overall: 12·677in (322mm).

4 Pullmore Car Transporter; DT No 582/982. A variant on model at (2).

5 Car Carrier; DT No 984, and Trailer, DT No 985, issued in July 1958 and in production until 1963. These two Supertoys models could be purchased separately or as a set (DT No 983); in the latter case, the models bore the decal "Dinky Toys Delivery Service" rather than "Dinky Auto Service" decals, as seen here. Both the Carrier and Trailer have hinged rear ramps; the Carrier has an adjustable-angle upper deck and the Trailer is

fitted with swivelling front wheels. In the DT No 983 Set finish, these models verge on scarcity; as separate items, the Carrier is limited and the Trailer fairly common. Lengths: (Carrier) 9·449in (240mm); (Trailer) 7·717in (196mm); (overall) 17·717in (450mm).

6 A.E.C. Fuel Tanker, "Esso"; DT No 945, issued in 1966 and available until 1967. Using the same cab as (3), this model may also be found with the "Esso Tiger" on its tank: the version shown is more common. Length: 10·472in (266mm).

7 A.E.C. Fuel Tanker, "Lucas Oil"; DT No 945 – the same as (6), but in a special finish as a promotional model for the Lucas company in 1977-78. A limited item.

8 Leyland Dump Truck; DT No 925, issued in 1967 and in production

until 1969. This model has a forward-tipping cab and a tipping body. It is of limited availability. Length: 7·559in (192mm).

9 Leyland Eight-Wheeled Chassis: DT No 936, issued in September 1964 and in production until 1969. This model of a test vehicle has the half-figure of a driver, a prop-shaft that turns and three removable (as seen) "5 Tons" weights on the body. It is a limited item. Length: 7·756in (197mm).

10 Mighty Antar Low Loader with Propeller; DT No 986, issued in June 1959 and in production until 1964. The six-wheeled tractor pulls a four-wheeled trailer on which is a ship's propeller in gold plastic. The same Thorneycroft tractor unit was used in military finish for the Tank Transporter (DT No 660, 1956-64);

see also (11). A limited item. Length: 12·008in (305mm).

11 Mighty Antar with Transformer; DT No 908, issued in October 1962 and in production until 1964. The Thorneycroft cab is the same as (10); the trailer incorporates a spare wheel and hinged rear ramps and carries a grey plastic transformer. A limited model. Length: 13·268in (337mm).

12 Leyland Comet Lorry; DT No 417. This is the renumbered version of DT No 531/931, see (13). The example shown has wheels with black rubber tyres and dates from 1956-59. It is a limited item. Length: 5·76in (144mm).

13 Leyland Comet Lorry; DT No 531; this is the original version of the model, issued in 1949, renumbered 931 in 1954, again renumbered

417 in 1956, and in production until 1959. It has Supertoys wheels of the earlier type, with grey rubber tyres. Limited. Length: as (12).

14 Leyland Comet Lorry with Hinged Tailboard; DT No 418, issued in January 1952 as DT No 532, renumbered 932 in 1954, again renumbered 418 in 1956, and available until 1959. The cab and chassis are the same as (12-13). Limited. Length: 5·591in (142mm).

15 Bedford TK Coal Wagon; DT No 425, issued in September 1964 and in production until 1967. As shown, it was sold complete with coal sacks and scales. Limited. Length: 4·764in (121mm).

16 Bedford TK Tipper; DT No 435, issued in May 1964 and in production until 1968. Appearing in various finishes, of which the

one shown is a later production example, it has a tipping body on which both sides and tailgate may be dropped down. Fairly common. Length: 4·724in (120mm).

17 Bedford TK Coca-Cola Truck with Crate Load; DT No 402, issued in 1966 and in production until 1969. Appearing only in this finish, the truck carries six plastic crates. The Bedford TK cab/chassis was used at this period in five different models; the only one not shown on this spread is the Crash Truck, which appears at (13-14), *pages 100-101*. Limited. Length: 4·764in (121mm).

18 Bedford TK Box Van, "Castrol"; DT No 450, issued in 1965 and in production until 1969. Appearing only in the finish shown, this has opening side doors. Fairly common. Length: 5·629in (143mm).

Diecast Vehicles by Dinky Toys, France, 1950s-1970s

1 Willème Covered Semi-Trailer (*Willème semi-remorque bâchée*) by Dinky Toys, France; French Dinky Toys Reference Number (FDT No) 36B, issued in 1958, renumbered 896 in 1959, and in production until 1971. The tractor unit was made in two forms, with straight or inclined chassis members. Appearing only in red, it is a one-piece casting and has double rear wheels, with a spare wheel at the rear of the cab. It is attached to the trailer by a sprung-steel clip device. The detachable trailer, in "wood" finish, has opening doors and a cover of soft green plastic. Like many French-made Dinky Toys, the availability of this model in Great Britain is generally limited. Length overall: 10·433in (265mm).

2 Unic Boilot Car Transporter (*Unic Boilot porte-voitures*); FDT No 39A, issued in November 1957, renumbered 894 in 1959, and in production until 1968. The Unic cab was used at this period, with casting variations, in several models. The large trailer, with single rear wheels, incorporates a mechanism for raising the top deck, activated by the crank-handle seen on its side. Note the spare wheel mounted on the front of the trailer. It bears "Dinky Toys Service Livraison" decals on its upper sides. It is possible that the cab may have been produced for a time with clear plastic windows. Limited. Length overall: 12·795in (325mm).

3 Saviem Metal Carrier (*Saviem Portefers*); FDT No 885, issued in 1966 and in production until 1971. This unusual model of a vehicle purpose-designed for carrying metal girders incorporates magnets to hold its load of metal strips in place. It is fitted with jewelled headlights; note also such details in plastic as the rear-view mirrors and warning light at the rear. The cab is fitted with sliding plastic doors and houses the plastic figure of a driver. Length: 8·74in (222mm).

4 Berliet Transformer Carrier (*Berliet Porte Transformateur*); FDT No 898, issued in June 1961 and in production until 1965. The tractor and trailer are civilian-finished versions of the Berliet Tank Transporter (*Porte char*), FDT No 890, a military model produced in 1959-70. The cab is fitted with clear plastic windows and the trailer has a spare wheel mounted at the front and is fitted with fold-down rear ramps. The "Alsthom" transformer, which houses its accessories in its hollow base, is made of grey plastic. Scarce. Length overall: 12·402in (315mm).

5 Unic Saharien Pipe-Line Transporter (*Unic Saharien Semi-remorque Pipeline*); DT No 39B, issued in 1959, immediately renumbered 893, and in production until 1960. It was also marketed in Great Britain in 1960-62. Note the two spare wheels at the rear of the cab, which is marked as a later production model by its clear plastic windows The trailer carries six black plastic pipes (sold separately) to make a pipe-line. Length overall: 8·858in (225mm).

6 Citroën P55 Milk Lorry (*Citroën P55 Laitier*); FDT No 586, issued in

74

July 1961 and in production until 1965. The cab is fitted with clear plastic windows and at the rear are thirty removable milk-bottle crates (not all are shown here) of grey-and-white plastic. A scarce model. Length: 6·969in (177mm).

7 Berliet GAK Tipper (*Berliet GAK Benne*); FDT No 585, issued in June 1961 and in production until 1964. The example shown is of the earlier type, 1961-62, with wide ribbing on its tipping rear; the later version, 1962-64, has narrower ribbing. Scarce. Length: 5·00in (127mm).

8 Willème Log-Carrier (*Willème Semi-remorque fardier*); FDT No 36A, issued in July 1956, renumbered 897 in 1959, and in production until 1960. The cab is the same as that described at (1), in this case articulated with a single-beam

trailer which has metal supports to retain a load of six "tree trunks". Length: 8·858in (225mm).

9 Unic Multi-Bucket Marrel (*Unic Multibenne Marrel*); FDT No 38A, issued in 1957, renumbered 895 in 1959, and in production until 1965. An earlier production model, without windows, is shown here. As is apparent in the photograph, the bucket swings out to dump its load. A limited item. Length: 5·197in (132mm).

10 Berliet Flat Truck with Container (*Berliet Plateau et Containeur*); FDT No 34B, issued in February 1956, renumbered 581 in 1959, and in production until 1965. The rear of the truck is cast with four slots to accommodate the diecast container, which has a lifting ring on its top and is fitted with a sliding

door. It is a limited item. Length: 4·921in (125mm).

11 Berliet Tipping Quarry Truck (*Berliet Benne basculante type carrière*); FDT No 34A, issued in October 1955, renumbered 580 in 1959, and in production until 1970. This model has the same cab and chassis as (10), but is fitted with a tipping rear body, without a tailboard, operated by a crank-handle that works a rack-and-pinion gear. Length: 5·039in (128mm).

12 Berliet Stradair Tipper Truck (*Berliet Stradair Benne basculante*); FDT No 569, issued in 1967 and in production until 1971. The cab is fitted with clear plastic windows and has a detailed interior; the bonnet opens to show a detailed engine. The body tips sideways, left and right, and has four hinged

flaps. Length: 6·889in (175mm).

13 Simca Cargo Van (*Simca Cargo fourgon*); FDT No 33A, issued in April 1955 and in production until 1956. It has opening rear doors. The model appeared first in olive-green-and-lemon, as shown, and then in green-and-orange. A limited item. Length: 5·236in (133mm).

14-15 Simca Cargo Tipper Truck (*Simca Cargo Benne basculante*); FDT No 33B, issued in July 1955, renumbered 578 in 1959, and in production until 1970. This model is fitted with a simple bent-wire-operated tipping system for its rear body. It appeared in various colour finishes. Early versions have a smooth rear body; later ones have a ribbed body, as seen in the example of the model at (14). Length: 5·00in (127mm).

Diecast Lorries and Vans by French Makers, 1950s-1970s

1 Unic Semi-Trailer "Air BP" (*Unic semi-remorque*) by Dinky Toys, France; French Dinky Toys Reference Number (FDT No) 887, issued in December 1963 and in production until 1971. This model features battery-powered headlights, with the simulated spare wheel to the rear of the cab acting as an on/off switch. The tank is provided with an automatically-descending stabilising leg; it is watertight and can be filled through the hatches on its top. Plastic hoses (not shown) are supplied to connect with the tank. Limited. Length: 12·047in (306mm).

2 Panhard Semi-Trailer "Esso" Tanker Titan (*Panhard semi-remorque Esso-citerne Titan*); FDT No 32C, issued in September 1954 and in production until 1959. Note the

chromed walk-way along the tank. The model may be found with large (early) or small (later) "Esso" decals. Limited. Length: 7·008in (178mm).

3 GMC and "Pinder" Trailer (*GMC et remorque "Pinder"*); FDT No 881, issued in 1969 and in production until 1971. The lorry and the four-wheeled trailer bear the decals of a famous European circus. The trailer has two sliding divisions between the cages and is fitted with twelve hinged side panels and a plastic roof. See (4). Limited. Length overall: 13·386in (340mm).

4 Peugeot 404 with "Pinder" Caravan (*Peugeot 404 avec caravane "Pinder"*); FDT No 882, issued in 1969 and in production until 1971. A companion to (3), this set consists of the Peugeot 404 (FDT No 536) and the Caravelair

Caravan (FDT No 564). The car has a plastic sign on its roof and the set contained also the plastic figure of a bear. It is a limited item. Length overall: 8·622in (219mm).

5 Unic S.N.C.F. Semi-Trailer (*Unic semi-remorque S.N.C.F.*); FDT No 803, issued in 1967 and in production until 1969. The cab has jewelled headlights and the trailer, with a slide-open rear panel, bears "S.N.C.F." and "Pam-Pam" stickers. This is a limited item. Length: 10·039in (255mm).

6 GMC 2½-Ton Timber Lorry with Trailer by F.J., France; dating from the 1960s. It is a limited item. Length overall: 7·48in (190mm).

7 GMC 2½-Ton Tipper Truck by F.J., France; dating from the 1960s. Limited. Length: 4·528in (115mm).

8 Saviem Horsebox with Racing

Sulky (*Saviem Goélette avec Sulky*); FDT No 571, issued in 1969 and in production until 1971. The horsebox has a detailed interior, two opening doors and a hinged ramp. The horse, jockey and sulky are plastic. Limited. Length (horsebox): 4·528in (115mm).

9 Renault Estafette Covered Pick Up (*Renault Estafette Pick Up bâché*); FDT No 563, issued in 1960 and in production until 1962. Note the green plastic canopy and removable spare wheel. A limited item. Length: 3·78in (96mm).

10 Panhard Semi-Trailer "Kodak" (*Panhard semi-remorque "Kodak"*); FDT No 32AJ, issued in 1952 and in production until 1953. Limited. Length: 6·496in (165mm).

11 Panhard Semi-Trailer "S.N.C.F." (*Panhard semi-remorque*

"S.N.C.F."); FDT No 32AB, issued in April 1954, renumbered 575, and in production until 1959. Like (10), it is fitted with a tinplate canopy. Limited. Length: 6·496in (165mm).

12 Unic Multibucket Double (*Unic Multibenne double*); FDT No 805, issued in 1966 and in production until 1971. With a lever-operated gear for swinging out its load, this model is supplied with two removable containers. Limited. Length: 5·197in (132mm).

13 Citroën 1200KG Van "Philips" (*Citroën 1200KG "Philips"*); FDT No 587, issued in 1964 and in production until 1970. Fitted with large clear plastic windows and with hinged panels at sides and rear, this has plastic "Philips" signs on either side of its roof. Limited. Length: 4·803in (122mm).

14 Berliet GAK Cattle Truck (*Berliet GAK Bétaillère*); FDT No 577, issued in July 1965 and in production until 1971. It has a plastic rear body with a hinged flap and was supplied complete with two plastic cows. A limited item. Length: 5·276in (134mm).

15 Peugeot "J 7 Allo-Frêt" Van (*Peugeot "J 7 Allo-Frêt"*); FDT No 570, issued in 1967 and in production until 1971. Limited. Length: 4·252in (108mm).

16 Simca Cargo Van "Bailly" (*Simca Cargo Fourgon "Bailly"*); FDT No 33AN, issued in 1956, renumbered 577, and in production until 1961. Limited. Length: 5·236in (133mm).

17 Simca Cargo Glazier's Van (*Simca Cargo Miroitier*); FDT No 33C, issued in October 1955, re-numbered 579, and in production until 1967. The rear is fitted with a tinplate frame to support a polished tinplate "mirror" and a plastic "window". A limited item. Length: 5·079in (129mm).

18-19 Citroën 1200KG Van "Cibié" (*Citroën 1200KG Camionette "Cibié"*); FDT No 25CG, issued in 1959, renumbered 561, and in production until 1963. Fitted with a sliding door, this is to be found with hubbed wheels (18) or, later, concave wheels (19). Limited. Length: 3·5625in (90mm).

20 Citroën 1200KG Van "Ch.Gervais"; FDT No 25CG, issued in June 1957, renumbered 561, and in production until 1959. Limited. Length: 3·5625in (90mm).

21 Citroën 1200KG Van "Glaces Gervais"; FDT No 561, issued in 1963 and in production until 1966.

Length: as (20).

22 Citroën 1200KG Metal Van (*Citroën 1200KG Camionette*); FDT No 25C, issued in June 1954 and in production until 1957. Limited. Length: 3·5625in (90mm).

23 Renault 1000KG Van "Correspondence S.N.C.F.", by CIJ, France; dating from the 1950s. It is a limited item. Length: 4·17in (106mm).

24 Peugeot Van "Lampe Mazda" (*Fourgon Peugeot "Lampe Mazda"*); FDT No 25B, issued in September 1953 and in production until April 1954. A scarce item. Length: 3·5625in (90mm).

25 Renault Estafette Glazier's Van (*Renault Estafette Miroitier*); FDT No 564, issued in 1963 and in production until 1965. Limited. Length: 3·78in (96mm).

1

2

3

7

8

9

10

13

14

15

1 Petrol Tanker, "Petrol", by Dinky Toys, Great Britain; Dinky Toys Reference Number (DT No) 30p. This model was first issued in 1952, appearing also with a green body, and remained in production until 1954. For some reason known only to the maker, this set of petrol tankers—of which further examples are shown at (2-5)—was modelled on an American Studebaker. The availability of this model is limited. Length: 4·409in (112mm).

2 Petrol Tanker, "Castrol"; DT No 441, first issued in 1954 and in production until 1960. This model was originally issued as DT No 30pa in 1952, remaining available under this number until 1954. In both cases, the model appeared only with a green body. The availabilty of both versions is

limited; however, the later version shown here may be a little harder to find. Length: 4·409in (112mm).

3 Petrol Tanker, "Mobilgas"; DT No 440, first issued in 1956 and in production until 1961. This model was originally issued as DT No 30p—the same number as the "Petrol" version shown at (1)—in 1952, remaining available under this number until 1954. In both cases the model appeared with a red body, but examples of DT No 440 produced after 1957 may have the "Mobilgas" decal with a white background. All versions are presently of limited availability. Length: 4·409in (112mm).

4 Petrol Tanker, "National Benzole Mixture"; DT No 443, first issued in 1957 and in production until 1958. This is the hardest to find of the

Studebaker-type tankers: it was produced only for a short period and only in the finish shown, with a yellow body and wheel hubs, silver trim, and lettering in black. Fairly scarce. Length: 4·409in (112mm).

5 Petrol Tanker, "Esso Motor Oil Petrol"; DT No 442, first issued in 1954 and available until 1960. This model was originally issued as DT No 30pb, appearing in 1952 and remaining available under this number until 1954. Both versions appeared with red body finish only, and both are of limited availability. Length: 4·409in (112mm).

6 Morris 10cwt Van, "Have a Capstan"; DT No 465, first issued in 1957 and in production until 1959. This model appeared only in the finish shown, with a body in two shades of blue, a silver radiator

and a cigarette motif. It is now quite scarce. Length: 3·071in (78mm).

7 Trojan 15cwt Van, "Chivers Jellies/Always turn out well"; DT No 31c, first issued in 1953 and in production until 1954, when it was renumbered DT No 452, remaining available under this number until 1957. Both versions appeared only in green body finish. The Trojans were the first "advertising vans" to be produced by Dinky Toys after World War II: the model appeared in six different logos, all of which are shown on this spread (7-12). All have one-piece diecast bodies and are fitted with tinplate baseplates. This model is of limited availability under both numbers. Length: 3·346in (85mm).

8 Trojan 15cwt Van, "Brooke Bond Tea"; DT No 455, first issued in

1957 and in production until 1961. See also note at (9). Limited. Length: 3·346in (85mm).

9 Trojan 15cwt Van, "Beefy Oxo"; DT No 31d, first issued in 1953 and in production until 1954. In the latter year this model was renumbered DT No 453, but was withdrawn within a few weeks to be replaced by the "Brooke Bond Tea" models shown at (8); possibly because of the real-life takeover of the Oxo company by Brooke Bond at that time. It is by far the hardest to find of the Trojan vans and must be described as very scarce. Length: 3·346in (85mm).

10 Trojan 15cwt Van, "Dunlop/The World's Master Tyre"; DT No 451, first issued in 1955 and in production until 1957. This model was originally issued as DT No

31b, appearing in 1952 and remaining available under this number until 1954. Both versions are of limited availability, but the earlier one may be harder to find. Length: 3·346in (85mm).

11 Trojan 15cwt Van, "Drink/Cydrax/ Sweet/Sparkling"; DT No 454, first issued in 1957 and in production until 1959. It is of limited availability. Length: 3·346in (85mm).

12 Trojan 15cwt Van, "Esso"; DT No 450, first issued in 1955 and in production until 1957. This model was originally issued as DT No 31a in 1951, remaining available under this number until 1954. Both versions are of limited availability. Length: 3·346in (85mm).

13 Austin Van, "Shell-BP"; DT No 470, first issued in 1954 and in production until 1956. This model

based on an Austin A40 10cwt van was produced by Dinky Toys with three advertising logos, all of which are shown on this spread (13-15). All appeared only in the finishes shown. Note that on this model the "Shell" decal is on the side nearest the camera; a "BP" decal appears on the other side, and both decals feature on the rear doors. Its availability is certainly limited. Length: 3·504in (89mm).

14 Austin Van, "Raleigh Cycles"; DT No 472, first issued in 1957 and in production until 1960. Limited. Length: 3·504in (89mm).

15 Austin Van, "Nestlé's"; DT No 471, first issued in 1955 and in production until 1960. Limited. Length: 3·504in (89mm).

16 Bedford Van, "Kodak/Cameras & Films"; DT No 480, first issued in

1954 and in production until 1956. This model based on a Bedford CA 10cwt van was made with three logos, all of which are shown on this spread (16-18). Limited availability. Length: 3·268in (83mm).

17 Bedford Van, "Ovaltine/& Ovaltine Biscuits"; DT No 481, first issued in 1955 and in production until 1960. Limited. Length: 3·268in (83mm).

18 Bedford Van, "Dinky Toys"; DT No 482, first issued in 1956 and in production until 1960. Limited. Length: 3·268in (83mm).

19 Bedford 12cwt Van, "Evening Standard", by Corgi Toys, Great Britain; maker's reference number 421. This model was first issued in 1960 and remained in production until 1962. It appeared only in the black, silver and red finish shown. Length: 3·268in (83mm).

1 Camping Caravan Caravelair 420 by Dinky Toys, France; French Dinky Toys Reference Number (FDT No) 564, in production 1969-71. The model has a detailed interior, clear plastic windows and a plastic tow-bar. Length: 5·315in (135mm).

2 Camping Caravan; FDT No 811, in production 1959-62. This model is fitted with a metal tow-bar. Length: 5·315in (135mm).

3-4 Caravan by Dinky Toys, Great Britain; Dinky Toys Reference Number (DT No) 190, issued in May 1956 and in production until 1960. It appeared in various two-tone finishes and is fitted with a metal tow-bar. Its tinplate base plate bears the maker's name, "190" and "Caravan". A common item. Length: 4·646in (118mm).

5-8 Four-Berth Caravan; DT No 188. This model was issued in April 1961 and remained in production in the form seen at (5) and (8), with a small sky-light and windows of clear plastic, a basically detailed interior and an opening plastic door, until 1963. In August 1963, the same casting was used for the version shown at (6) and (7), which had a transparent roof and larger end windows. This had the DT No 117, but was sold in the same box as DT No 188, with a "117" sticker. It was available thus until 1969. Both versions are fairly common; the earlier one may be harder to find. Length: 5·197in (132mm).

9 Caravan Trailer; DT No 30g, issued in April 1936 and in production until 1940 — the only "30 Series" vehicle not to be reissued post-War. It is a one-piece casting and is fitted with a wire tow-bar. It appeared in various two-tone finishes and may be found with the roof-lights voided, as seen, or filled in. Note the grey rubber tyres. This is now a fairly scarce item. Length: 3·189in (81mm).

10-11 Four-Wheeled Hand Truck; DT No 105c, issued in June 1949, renumbered 383 in 1954, and in production until 1958. This model in Dinky Toys Farm and Garden range appeared in green (11) in 1949-54, and blue (10) in 1954-58. It has swivelling front wheels and is fitted with a towing-hook. It has metal wheels. Common. Length (with handle): 4·961in (126mm).

12 Healey Sports Boat on Trailer; DT No 796, issued in September 1960 and in production until 1967. The boat is plastic, with windscreen and steering wheel; the trailer is diecast, with plastic wheels. Fairly common. Lengths (boat): 3·70in (94mm); (trailer) 3·858in (98mm).

13 Renault Estafette Camping by Dinky Toys, France; FDT No 565, in production 1965-71. It has a detailed interior and a sliding side door. Length: 3·66in (93mm).

14-15 Loudspeaker Van; DT No 34c, issued in February 1948, renumbered 492 in 1954, and in production until 1957. This is a one-piece third-type "28 Series" van casting with un-voided rear windows; it has a diecast speaker unit mounted on the roof. It appeared in various colours, two of which are shown. Fairly common. Length: 3·189in (81mm).

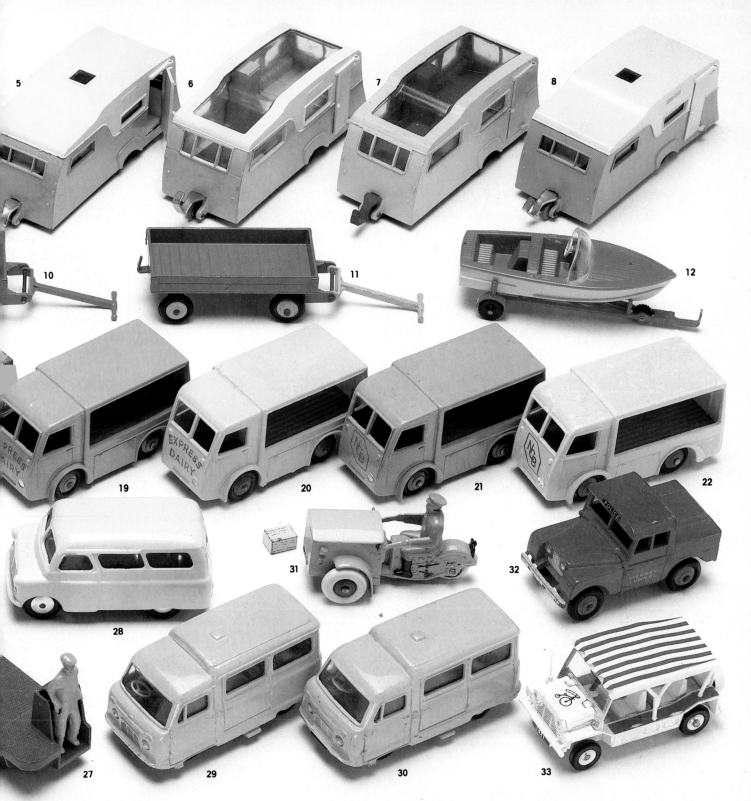

16 Delivery Van; DT No 280, issued in 1948 and in production until 1954. The same casting as (14-15), this appeared in red or blue. Note that DT No 280 was later used for an Observation Coach (1954-60). Fairly common. Length: 3·189in (81mm).

17-22 Electric Dairy Van; DT No 30v. This model was first issued in 1949 in the form shown at (21) and (22), with "NCB" decal. The version with "Express Dairy" decal, shown at (18) and (20), first appeared in 1951, and the promotional model with "Job's Dairy" decal (17) in 1953. In 1954, the "Express Dairy" version was renumbered 490 and the "NCB" and "Job's Dairy" versions became No 491. It is believed that the later "NCB" version was intended for sale overseas. The "Express Dairy" version is fairly common; "NCB" will be harder to find; "Job's Dairy" is limited, verging on scarce. Length: 3·346in (85mm).

23 "Pathe News" Camera Car; DT No 281, issued in 1968 and in production until 1970. The Fiat 2300 Station Wagon on which the cameraman and camera are mounted has clear plastic windows, a detailed interior and opening bonnet, doors and tailgate. It appeared only in black. Common. Length: 4·252in (108mm).

24 "Radio Telé/Luxembourg" Camera Car, Citroën ID 19 Shooting Brake, by Dinky Toys, France; FDT No 1404, dating from the early 1970s. Length: 4·528in (115mm).

25-27 B.E.V. Electric Truck; DT No 14a, issued in July 1948, renumbered 400 in 1954, and in production until 1960. Fitted with a diecast driver and a towing-hook, this model will be easy to find. Length: 3·346in (85mm).

28 Bedford Dormobile by Corgi Toys, Great Britain; maker's reference number 404, issued in 1956 and in production until 1962. Appearing in various colours, this model is fairly common, but a version with friction drive, made in 1956-59, is scarce. Length: 3·268in (83mm).

29-30 Atlas Kenebrake Bus; DT No 295, issued in May 1960 and in production until 1964. Normally appearing in light-blue-and-grey (30), it is shown here with a colour variant (29). This was the first Dinky Toys vehicle to feature a detailed interior and the first Dinky bus with clear plastic windows. It also features suspension. Fairly common. Length: 3·386in (86mm).

31 Three-Wheeled Delivery Van (*Triporteur*) by Dinky Toys, France; FDT No 14z, in production 1937-40. The box has an opening lid. It was available in Britain from 1938 onward. A limited item. Length: 2·756in (70mm).

32 Mersey Tunnel Police Van; DT No 255, issued in September 1955 and in production until 1961. Appearing only in red, it has a towing-hook. A common item. Length: 3·031in (77mm).

33 "Prisoner" Mini-Moke; DT No 106, issued in 1967 (as a tie-in with the popular TV series, "The Prisoner") and in production until 1970. It appeared only in the finish shown. It is a fairly common model. Length: 2·874in (73mm).

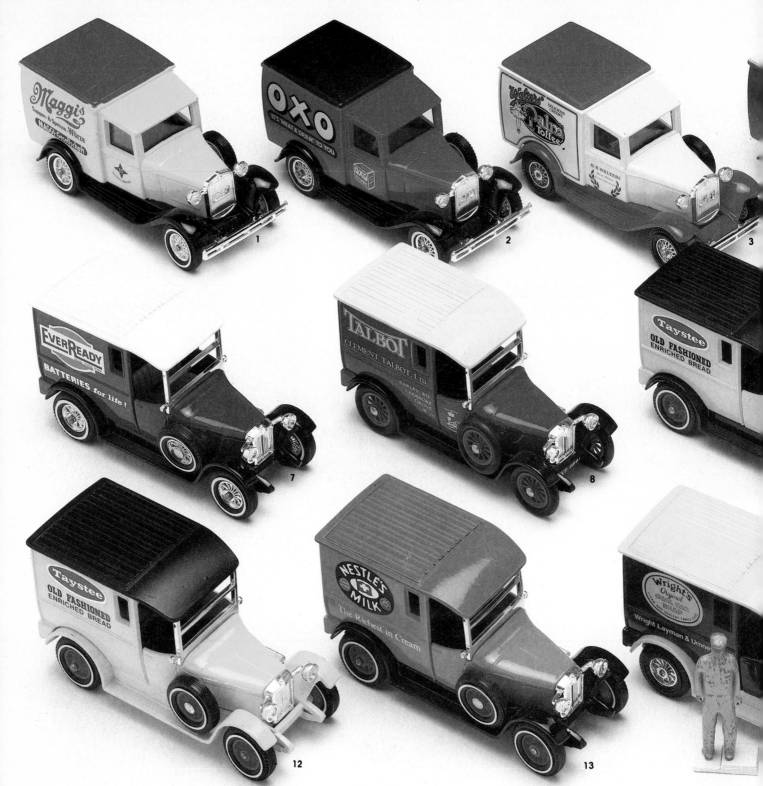

1 ... 7 ... 8

12 ... 13

1 1930 Ford Model "A" Van, "Maggi Soups", by Lesney, Great Britain; Models of Yesteryear (MoY) Y-22 (1st Issue; second type). First appearing in 1983, this model is currently available. A variation in finish on (2), this van bears the Maggi company's advertising in the German language; a version in the same yellow and red finish, but with English-language advertising, is harder to find. A common item. Length: 4·016in (102mm).

2 1930 Ford Model "A" Van, "Oxo/It's Meat & Drink To You"; MoY Y-22 (1st Issue; first type). First appearing in 1982 and currently available, this model may be found with its black roof in either rough or smooth finish. Like (1), it has silver plastic spoked wheels with whitewall tyres. A common

item. Length: 4·016in (102mm).
3 1930 Ford Model "A" Van, "Walters' Delicious Creemy (sic)/Palm Toffee"; MoY Y-22 (1st Issue; third type).First appearing in 1984 and currently available, this model is a further variation on (1) and (2); it is fitted with gold plastic spoked wheels without whitewalls. Common. Length: 4·016in (102mm).
4 1930 Ford Model "A" Van, "Ever Ready/Batteries/for longer life!"; first appearing in 1984 and still available. A further variation on (1), (2) and (3), again with silver plastic spoked wheels and whitewall tyres. For a similarly-finished "Ever Ready" van—but a quite different model—see (7). A common item. Length: 4·016in (102mm).
5 1930 Ford Model "A" Van, "Toblerone"; MoY Y-22 (1st Issue;

fifth type), first appearing in 1985 and currently available. At the time of writing (Spring 1985), this was the most recent variation in finish in the Model "A" range. Common. Length: 4·016in (102mm).
6 Ford Model "A" Woody Wagon, "A & J Box/General Stores"; MoY Y-21 (1st Issue; third type). This variation first appeared in 1983 and is currently available. The first type of Woody Wagon (so called from its wood-panelled body) appeared in 1981, with a yellow body, dark brown chassis and black roof; the second type, appearing in 1982, has a yellow body, black chassis and black roof. All three types are common; the earlier ones may be a little harder to find. Length: 3·937in (100mm).
7 1927 Talbot Van, "Ever Ready/

Batteries for life!"; MoY Y-5 (4th Issue; tenth type). This variation in finish in the large Talbot Van range first appeared in 1983 and is currently available. The tan seats of this example mark it as the first issue of its type; a second issue, with black seats, appeared in the same year. Both are common. Length: 3·74in (95mm).
8 1927 Talbot Van, "Talbot"; MoY Y-5 (4th Issue; unidentified type). This version, which carries advertising for the maker of the prototype vehicle, has artillery-type wheels of the early pattern: of large diameter and fitted with smooth plastic tyres. It is thought to be of limited availability. Length: 3·74in (95mm).
9 1927 Talbot Van, "Taystee/Old Fashioned/Enriched Bread"; MoY

Y-5 (4th Issue; fourth type). The type first appeared in 1980; however, the black chassis of this example marks it as the colour-change version that appeared in 1981. For the original version, see (12). The version shown here is not currently available; it remains quite common, but (12) will prove easier to find. Length: 3·74in (95mm).

10 1927 Talbot Van, "Ibcam Motoring Festival/August 23, 25, 25, 1980"; MoY Y-5 (4th Issue; unidentified type). A "Models of Yesteryear" van with appropriate paintwork and decals is specifically issued each year for sale at this British festival for motor enthusiasts. The models are always dated, like the example shown, and are fairly eagerly sought by all collectors. Length 3·74in (95mm).

11 1927 Talbot Van, "Dunlop/Tyres & Accessories"; MoY Y-5 (4th Issue; unidentified type). This version of the Talbot Van appears to be unlisted. It may be a limited edition, in which case it will be a scarce item and very collectable. Length: 3·74in (95mm).

12 1927 Talbot Van, "Taystee/Old Fashioned/Enriched Bread"; MoY Y-5 (4th Issue; fourth type). See note at (9): this is the first version, marked as such by its yellow chassis, which first appeared in 1980 and is currently available. Note that a version with yellow body and yellow chassis, with the word "Taystee" in yellow on red (as compared to white on red in the British versions shown), was made for sale in the USA. Two other yellow-finished Talbot vans (4th

Issue; fifth and sixth types), with advertising for "Merita Old Fashioned Enriched Bread" and "Langendorf Old Fashioned Enriched Bread", were made only to be sold on the US market. Length: 3·74in (95mm).

13 1927 Talbot Van, "Nestlé's Milk/ The Richest in Cream"; MoY Y-5 (4th Issue; seventh type). This version first appeared in 1981; it is not currently available and is among the hardest to find of the Talbot vans. Even more difficult to obtain (outside its intended marketing area) is a version with a lighter grey roof, issued in the same year for the Australian market. Limited. Length: 3·74in (95mm).

14 1927 Talbot Van, "Wright's/ Original/Coal Tar/Soap"; MoY Y-5 (4th Issue; ninth type). This version

first appeared in 1982 and is currently available. It may be found with either silver (as shown) or gold plastic spoked wheels. Common. Length: 3·74in (95mm).

15 1927 Talbot Van, "Chivers/&/Sons Ltd./Jams, Jellies & Marmalades"; MoY Y-5 (4th Issue; eighth type). This version first appeared in 1982 and is currently available. Common. Length: 3·74in (95mm).

16 1927 Talbot Van, "Chocolat/ Menier"; MoY Y-5 (4th Issue; second type). This was the first variation to appear on the original Talbot van (which bore "Lipton's Tea" advertising; with the words "By Appointment", which were replaced by the firm's address in 1980), and was issued in the same year, 1978. It is currently available. Common. Length: 3·74in (95mm).

1 1912 Ford Model "T" Tanker, "Carnation/Farm Products", by Lesney, Great Britain; Models of Yesteryear (MoY) Y-3 (4th Issue; fourth type). This version of the Model "T" tanker first appeared in 1984 and is currently available. Note that unlike the other versions of this model it is fitted with whitewall tyres. It is a common item. (The rarest of the Model "T" tankers, not shown here, is the "Zerolene/Standard Oil Company" tanker, issued in 1982, which had a green body and tank and was fitted with either red or gold plastic spoked wheels; any example of this version will be difficult to find.) Length: 3·898in (99mm).

2 1912 Ford Model "T" Tanker, "Guinness"; Moy Y-3 (4th Issue; fifth type). At the time of writing, this

was the most recent version, appearing in 1985 and currently available. Length: 3·898in (99mm).

3 1912 Ford Model "T" Tanker, "B.P."; MoY Y-3 (4th Issue; first type). This was the first of the Model "T" tankers, appearing in 1981. The example shown, with red plastic spoked wheels, is currently available; it may be found with or without black-shaded edging on the "B.P." lettering. A variant with gold plastic spoked wheels is much less common. Length: 3·898in (99mm).

4 1912 Ford Model "T" Tanker, "Express Dairy"; MoY Y-3 (4th Issue; third type). This version of the Model "T" tanker first appeared in 1983 and is currently available. Common. Length: 3·898in (99mm).

5 1910 Renault Type AG Van,

"Perrier/Mise En Bouteille A La/ Source Vergeze (Gard)/France"; MoY Y-25 (1st Issue). Appearing in 1983 and currently available, this attractive model with a body and chassis in contrasting shades of green features a spare wheel and a roof rack. No variations in finish of this van have yet appeared. Length: 3·937in (100mm).

6 1912 Ford Model "T" Van, "The/Hoover/It Beats . . ./as it Sweeps . . ./as it Cleans . . ." (and note the American-style spelling in the legend on the door: "Save time & labor"); MoY Y-12 (3rd Issue; thirteenth type). This version of the Model "T" van, to date the most prolific of all the "Yesteryear" models, appeared in 1983, the year which marked the 75th anniversary of both the Hoover

company and the Ford Model "T". It is currently available. Common. Length: 3·583in (91mm).

7 1912 Ford Model "T" Van, "Pepsi-Cola"; MoY Y-12 (3rd Issue; fourteenth type). It was presumably inevitable that with a "Coca-Cola" version—see (13)— appearing early in this range, that company's great rival should also require representation! This version first appeared in 1984 and is therefore currently available. Length: 3·583in (91mm).

8 1912 Ford Model "T" Van, "Bird's/Custard Powder"; MoY Y-12 (3rd Issue; seventh type). This version first appeared in 1982 and is currently available. A variant has appeared with tan seats (as opposed to black in the example shown) and with cast in rear doors

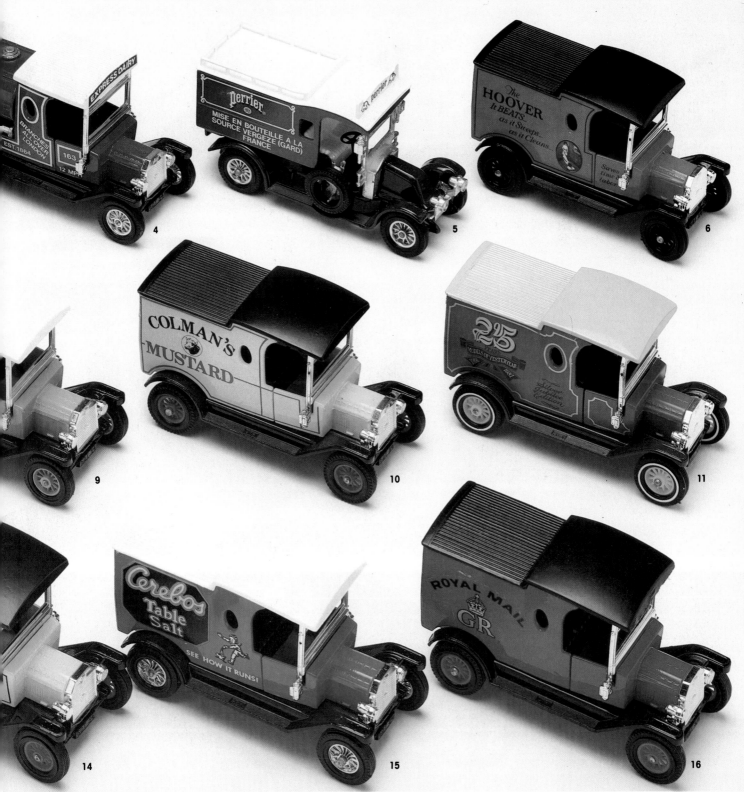

(as opposed to doors with a double line); this will be a little harder to find than the example shown, which is a common item. Length: 3·583in (91mm).

9 1912 Ford Model "T" Van, "Ovaltine/for/Health"; MoY Y-12 (3rd Issue; fifteenth type). At the time of writing, this was the latest to appear in the Model "T" range, presumably marking the 75th anniversary of the Ovaltine company in 1985. (A similar model, in the more familiar Ovaltine colours of orange and buff, was issued at around the same time in the "Days Gone" series of small diecast models made by Lledo (London) Ltd.) This model is currently available. Length: 3·583in (91mm).

10 1912 Ford Model "T" Van, "Colman's/Mustard"; MoY Y-12 (3rd Issue; first type). This was the first version of the Model "T" van, appearing in 1979. It is to be found with either a single or double line on the rear doors; both versions are common. Length: 3·583in (91mm).

11 1912 Ford Model "T" Van, "25/Years/Models of Yesteryear/ 1956/1981/ Silver Jubilee Edition"; MoY Y-12 (3rd Issue; fourth type). This version was issued in 1981 to mark the 25th anniversary of the "Models of Yesteryear" range. It is currently available in toyshops. Length: 3·583in (91mm).

12 1912 Ford Model "T" Van, "Captain/Morgan" ("Black Label Rum" on door); MoY Y-12 (3rd Issue; twelfth type). This version was first issued in 1983. It is to be found with its inscriptions applied either by decals or stickers; both variants are currently available and common. Length: 3·583in (91mm).

13 1912 Ford Model "T" Van, "Enjoy/Coca-Cola"; MoY Y-12 (3rd Issue; second type). This version, which appeared in 1979, was made for the American market. It is not easily found in Great Britain. A limited item. Length: 3·583in (91mm).

14 1912 Ford Model "T" Van, "Suze/A La Gentiane"; MoY Y-12 (3rd Issue; third type). This version first appeared in 1980. It is to be found with rear doors of either single- or double-line type; both variants are currently available and common. Length: 3·583in (91mm).

15 1912 Ford Model "T" Van, "Cerebos/Table/Salt/See How It Runs!"; MoY Y-12 (3rd Issue;

eighth type). This version first appeared in 1982; it is currently available and common. Length: 3·583in (91mm).

16 1912 Ford Model "T" Van, "Royal Mail/G.R." (with crown insignia); MoY Y-12 (3rd Issue; eleventh type). This first appeared in 1983 and is currently available. There are four other Model "T" vans that are not shown: "Smith's Potato Crisps" (fifth type), issued in 1982 for Australia and scarce in Britain; "Harrods/Express Delivery/ Motor Accessories" (ninth type), issued 1982, with three variants (double-line door; cast in door and black seats; tan seats), limited; and "Sunlight Seife" (tenth type), issued in 1982 for West Germany and limited in Great Britain. Length: 3·583in (91mm).

1 Double Decker Bus by Dinky Toys,
Great Britain; Dinky Toys Reference
Number (DT No) 290. The
perennially-popular double decker
was first issued early in 1938 as DT
No 29c – see (5), (8), (9) and (13).
It was reissued after World War II,
passing through several design
changes, as detailed below, and
being renumbered DT No 290 in
1955. It remained in production
under this number until 1963. The
example shown here, finished in
green-and-cream, and also
produced in red-and-cream, is
without a "number box" on the
front of its roof, marking it as one
produced between c1956, when
this feature was deleted – see (2),
and 1960, when it was reintroduced.
It bears the commonest of the
advertising transfers found on this

model: "Dunlop The World's Master
Tyre". The Leyland radiator seen
on this example featured on models
produced between 1948 and
1962. This model is fitted with spun-
aluminium wheels with rubber tyres.
Limited. Length: 4·055in (103mm).
2 Double Decker Bus; DT No 290.
This example is without the roof
box; see note at (1). Notice also
that the lettering of "Dunlop" is
upright, not slanted as at (1). It has
the Leyland radiator and, like the
examples shown at (3-9), is fitted
with ridged cast wheels with
rubber tyres. It is a limited item.
Length: 4·055in (103mm).
3 Double Decker Bus; DT No 290.
This example has the second-type
AEC radiator (also called the "Guy"
radiator); note that the "V" at the top
of the radiator is less pronounced

than at (5) and (9). This radiator
was fitted between 1950 and
c1956. Limited. Length: as (1).
4 Double Decker Bus; DT No 290.
This example, with roof box, is fitted
with the Leyland radiator. Limited.
Length: 4·055in (103mm).
5 Double Decker Bus; DT No 29c.
This is an earlier model with the
first-type AEC radiator – note the
pronounced "V" at the top of the
grille – fitted in the period 1949-59.
Limited. Length: 3·937in (100mm).
6 Double Decker Bus; DT No 290. In
red-and-cream finish, this has the
Leyland-type radiator. Limited.
Length: 4·055in (103mm).
7 Double Decker Bus; DT No 290.
This example has the second-type
AEC radiator. A limited item.
Length: 4·055in (103mm).
8 Double Decker Bus; DT No 29c. A

somewhat earlier example than (7),
dating from before the renumbering
of 1955, but again with the second-
type AEC radiator. A limited item.
Length: 3·937in (100mm).
9 Double Decker Bus; DT No 29c.
This is in the alternative colour
finish of red-and-grey and is fitted
with the first-type AEC radiator with
the pronounced "V". Limited.
Length: 3·937in (100mm).
10 Double Decker Bus; DT No 290.
This example is fitted with the
Leyland radiator and has aluminium
wheels. Limited. Length: as (1).
11 Double Decker Bus; DT No 291.
This model, based on the Leyland
version of No 290, was introduced
in 1959 and remained in production
until 1963. Finished in red, it bears
yellow-and-black "Exide Batteries"
decals. The example seen here is

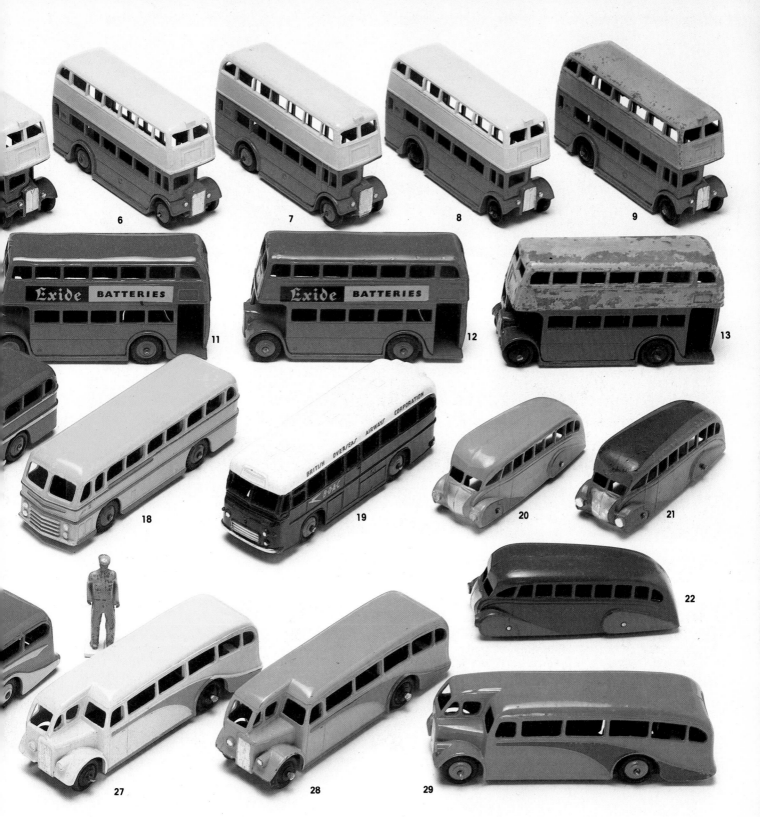

fitted with plastic wheels. Note that the same DT No was used for the Atlantean City Bus of 1974-77; see (15-17), *pages 90-91*. Limited. Length: 4·055in (103mm).

12 Double Decker Bus; DT No 291. As (11), but with ridged cast wheels. Limited. Length: 4·055in (103mm).

13 Double Decker Bus; DT No 29c. A side-view of this model, showing a two-tone green finish: other colour variations may be found. Limited. Length: 3·937in (100mm).

14 Observation Coach, DT No 280. This model was in production from 1954 to 1960; see (15). This one is the post-renumbering version, which appeared in cream with a red flash. It is a limited item. Length: 4·409in (112mm).

15 Observation Coach; DT no 29f. The original form of the model at

(14), first issued in 1950 and in production, in grey with red flash, until it was renumbered 280 in 1954. It may be a little harder to find than (14). Length: as (14).

16-18 Duple Roadmaster Coach; this model was first issued as DT No 29h in 1952, appearing in blue-and-silver, as shown at (16), until 1954. It was then renumbered 282, and remained in production, appearing in red-and-silver (17) and then yellow-and-red (18), until 1960. On later versions, the words "Leyland Royal Tiger" appear on the base plate. The blue- and red-and-silver versions are limited; the yellow-and-red version is scarce. Length: 4·6875in (119mm).

19 B.O.A.C. Coach; DT No 283. This was issued in 1956 and remained in production until 1963. Finished

in blue, with a white roof, it has the decal "British Overseas Airways Corporation" along its upper body, and "B.O.A.C.", with logo, on its side. It is a limited item. Length: 4·724in (120mm).

20-22 Streamline Bus; DT No 29b. This model was first issued in 1936, was in production until 1940, and was reissued in 1948-50. The body is a single casting and, unlike some other Dinky models, it is very rare to find pre-War examples that have been affected by metal fatigue. The major difference between pre- and post-War examples is that the former have a cut-out rear window and the latter have not. The model was made in various two-tone finishes additional to those of the post-War examples shown here.

Post-War versions are limited. Length: 3·465in (88mm).

23-26 Luxury Coach; DT No 29g (renumbered 281). This model was first issued in 1951 and was in production as No 29g, finished in cream with orange flashes, as seen at (25), until 1954. It was then re-named the Modern Coach, renumbered 281, and remained in production until 1960. It is a limited item. Length: 4·449in (113mm).

27-29 Single Deck Bus; DT No 29e. This model was first issued in 1948 and remained in production until 1952. It appeared only in the three colour finishes shown here: cream with blue flash (27); green with dark green flash (28); blue with dark blue flash (29). Limited. Length: 4·449in (113mm).

1 Berliet Urban Bus (*Berliet Bus urbain*) by Dinky Toys, France; French Dinky Toys Reference Number (FDT No) 889U, issued in 1965 and in production until 1970. Finished in the red-and-cream livery of T.C.L. de Lyon, this model features—as may be seen in the similar model shown at (2)— automatically-opening side doors (operating when the model is pressed firmly downwards), clear plastic windows and a detailed interior. It is fitted with jewelled headlights. It bears a "Pepsi-Cola" decal on the left side and, again as visible at (2), a "Dunlop" decal on the right. Like most models by Dinky Toys, France, it is of limited availability in Great Britain. Length: 8·819in (224mm).

2 Berliet Paris Bus (*Berliet Autobus Parisien*); FDT No 889, issued in 1965 and in production until 1970. Finished in the two-tone green livery of the R.A.T.P., this is in all other respects the same model as that shown at (1), bearing the same decals and here photographed from such an angle as to display more fully its various special features. Limited. Length: 8·819in (224mm).

3 Continental Touring Coach by Dinky Toys, Great Britain; Dinky Toys Reference Number (DT No) 953, issued in January 1963 and in production until 1965. This Dinky Supertoys models is fitted with clear plastic windows and has a detailed interior. It bears "Dinky Continental Tours" decals along its upper sides, and appeared only in pale-blue-and-white. Scarce. Length: 7·677in (195mm).

4 Vega Major Coach; DT No 961, issued in 1973 and in production until 1977. This most attractive model was issued for sale in Switzerland, and bears the appropriate finish; see (5) for the British version. It features battery-powered side-mounted indicator lights that flash when the six-wheeled vehicle is steered to the appropriate side by pressing down on its front (bogey) pair of wheels. It has opening doors and an opening rear luggage compartment; its clear plastic windows include roof-lights. Suspension is fitted. This model is of limited availability. Length: 9·528in (242mm).

5 Vega Major Luxury Coach; DT No 954, issued in 1972 and in production until 1976. This is basically the same model as that shown at (4), but in white finish with a maroon flash, as issued for the British market. Although plastic-lensed indicators are fitted on the sides, they do not flash on this model. On an earlier version— DT No 952, issued in 1964 and in production until 1971; now of limited availability—flashing lights as described at (4) were fitted. The earlier version was finished in grey with a maroon flash. The version shown here is a fairly common item. Length: 9·528in (242mm).

6 Wayne "School Bus"; DT No 949, issued in February 1961 and in production until 1964. Judging from its finish, it is probable that this Dinky Supertoys model was intended to be marketed in the United States, although it was in fact available only in Great Britain. It

has a detailed interior with a separate steering wheel (left-hand drive) and is fitted with clear plastic windows. Its tinplate base plate is stamped with the maker's name and "Wayne Bus". Limited. Length: 7·677in (195mm).

7 Renault Autobus by CIJ, France; dating from the early 1960s. The casting incorporates a roof rack. Limited. Length: 4·921in (125mm).

8 "Red Arrow" Single-Decker Bus; DT No 283, issued in 1971 and in production until 1976. Appearing at first in red finish and later in metallic red, this model is fitted with clear plastic windows, a number plate, a detailed interior, and opening side doors that are worked by a sliding-catch (just visible on the upper side of the vehicle away from the camera) that

also rings a bell. Fairly common. Length: 6·575in (167mm).

9 Mercedes Benz 18-Seater Coach (*Mercedes Benz Autocar 18 places*); FDT No 541, issued in May 1963 and in production until 1971. This model features clear plastic windows, including roof-lights, a detailed interior, and suspension. A limited model. Length: 4·409in (112mm).

10-11 Isobloc Coach (*Isobloc Autocar*); FDT No 29E, issued in 1953 and in production until March 1955. See also (12-13): this is the later version of the model, marked as such by the ribbing on the luggage-rack roof. As in all versions, the ladder at the rear is tinplate. It appeared only in the finishes shown. Limited. Length: 5·00in (127mm).

12-13 Isobloc Coach; FDT No 27E,

issued in 1951 and in production until 1952. An earlier version, with the same number, of the model at (10-11): note the smooth roof. Limited. Length: 5·00in (127mm).

14-15 Chausson Coach (*Chausson Autocar*); FDT No 29F, issued in April 1956, renumbered 571 in 1959, and in production until 1960. This well-detailed model was issued only in the two finishes shown. It is a limited item. Length: 6·063in (154mm).

16 Chausson Trolley Bus by Solido, France; maker's reference number AP52, issued in 1952 and available until 1957. Note the similarity in finish with the French Dinky Toys model shown at (14-15). Limited. Length: 5·591in (142mm).

17 Chausson Coach by Solido, France; issued in 1952 and available until

1957. The same casting is used as in the trolley bus at (16). Limited. Length: 5·591in (142mm).

18 Somua-Panhard Paris Bus (*Autobus parisien Somua-Panhard*); FDT No 29D, issued in January 1952 and renumbered 570 in 1959; production ceased in 1959 but this very popular model remained available until 1961. Limited. Length: 5·629in (143mm).

19 "Midland Red" Motorway Express Coach by Corgi Toys, Great Britain; maker's reference number 1120, issued in 1961 and in production until 1978. Bearing "Derby Birmingham Liverpool" route-board decals on its upper sides, this model has clear plastic windows and an interior with detail that extends even to a lavatory. A limited item. Length: 5·512in (140mm).

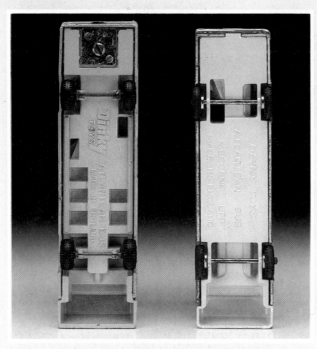

Left: *Closeup views of the undersides of two Atlantean bus models by Dinky Toys, Great Britain. On the right is an early example, with a simple white diecast chassis and metal wheels with rubber tyres. The later example (left) has a more complex yellow diecast chassis and is fitted with plastic speedwheels.*

1 Routemaster Double Decker Bus, "Queen's Silver Jubilee", by Corgi Toys, Great Britain; maker's reference number (MRN) 471, issued in 1977. This model has an all-silver body with the decals "See More London", printed in red against a London skyline in black, on its upper body, and "The Queen's Silver Jubilee/London Celebrations", with logo, in black on silver, on its lower body. Like all the Corgi Routemaster models shown on this spread (1–6), it has a plastic chassis and is fitted with plastic whizzwheels. It is fairly common. Length: 4·8425in (123mm).

2 Routemaster Double Decker Bus, "Disneyland", by Corgi Toys; MRN 470, dating from 1977. The open-topped Routemaster model first appeared in 1973, when

versions were issued bearing advertising on behalf of "Old Hoborn" (No C469/10, finished in orange); "Blackpool Transport" (No C469/17, finished in cream-and-green); "Manchester United" (No C469/23, finished in red); "Bournemouth" (No C469/30, finished in either orange or yellow); and "Suntrekker" (No C478, finished in orange-and-white). This version, finished in yellow with "Disneyland" in red, has a decal showing Walt Disney's famous cartoon characters along its upper body. A fairly common item. Length: 4·8425in (123mm).

3 Routemaster Double Decker Bus, "Swan & Edgar" "London Transport", by Corgi Toys; MRN C469, issued in 1974 and in production until 1980. Finished in

red, it bears the decal "Swan & Edgar Piccadilly Circus" on its upper side, and "London Transport" on its lower side. As on the models shown at (4) and (5), the headboards bear Corgi Toys' name and logo. A fairly common item. Length: 4·8425in (123mm).

4 Routemaster Double Decker Bus, "BTA" (British Travel Association) "London Transport", by Corgi Toys; MRN C469, the same as (3), issued in 1975 and currently available. The decal on the upper side reads "BTA Welcome to Britain", with a Union Flag motif; otherwise the finish is as (3). This model is common—but a variant bearing a label advertising the James Bond film "Octopussy", on one side only, is extremely rare. Length: 4·8425in (123mm).

5 Routemaster Double Decker Bus, "Selfridges" "London Transport", by Corgi Toys; MRN 467, first issued in 1977 and in production until 1981. The decal on the upper side reads: "There's no place like Selfridges", otherwise the the finish is as (3) and (4)—but note that this model has a Route 12 destination board, whereas (3) and (4) are Route 11. It is fairly common. Length: 4·8425in (123mm).

6 Routemaster Double Decker Bus, "Leeds" "Omnibus", by Corgi Toys; MRN C469, the same as (3) and (4), first issued in 1979 and in production until 1981. Finished in dark green and yellow, this bears the decal "Say 'the Leeds' and you're smiling" on the upper side, and "Omnibus", "George Shillibeer 1829 London Transport 1979"

(marking the 150th anniversary of the London bus service) on the lower side. It is one of the less common Routemaster models. Length: 4·8425in (123mm).

7-8 London Routemaster Bus, "Esso Safety Grip tyres", by Dinky Toys, Great Britain; Dinky Toys Reference Number (DT No) 289, first issued in 1970 and in production until 1977. In the familiar red finish of "London Transport", this model was produced with plastic speed-wheels, as shown at (7), or with aluminium wheels fitted with rubber tyres, as shown at (8). Both are fairly common, although the rubber-tyred version will probably be harder to find. Other "advertising" versions of DT No 289 include "Tern Shirts For Crispness" (1964-65); "Ssschweppes" (1965-

69); "Festival of London Stores" (c1970; a scarce item); and "Visit Madame Tussaud's" (1977-78). Length: 4·764in (121mm).

9 Atlantean Bus, "BP" "Corporation Transport", by Dinky Toys; DT No 293, first issued in 1963 and in production until 1968. Finished in green-and-white, this bears the decal "BP Is The Key To Better Motoring" on its upper side. Note that it incorporates the figure of a driver. It is of limited availability. Length: 4·764in (121mm).

10 Atlantean Bus, "Ribble", by Dinky Toys; DT No 292, first issued in 1962 and in production until 1966. Finished in red-and-white, this has "Regent for peak pulling power" on its upper side, and "Ribble" on its lower side. A limited item. Length: 4·764in (121mm).

11 Atlantean Bus, "Regent", by Dinky Toys; DT No 292: produced under the same number as (10), from 1962 until 1968, and the same model, save for the fact that "Corporation Transport" and a coat-of-arms replace "Ribble". Limited. Length: 4·764in (121mm).

12 Silver Jubilee Bus (Leyland Atlantean) by Dinky Toys; DT No 297, issued in 1977. Finished in silver, this bears the decal "The Queen's Silver Jubilee 1977" along the upper side, and "National" on the lower side. It has a diecast chassis and is fitted with plastic speedwheels. Fairly common; although a version specially-decalled for Woolworths stores is limited. Length: 4·764in (121mm).

13-14 Atlantean Bus, "Yellow Pages", by Dinky Toys; DT No 295. There

are several variants of this model. Two are shown here: (13) is in yellow with a white engine cover; (14) is finished overall in deeper yellow. The major variant is in the earlier versions, in production 1973-74, in which the lettering on the headboards is reversed; later versions, in production 1974-76, are lettered as seen at (14). The earlier version is fairly limited. Length: 4·8425in (123mm).

15-17 Atlantean City Bus, "Kenning", by Dinky Toys; DT No 291, issued in 1974 and in production until 1977. Three colour variants are shown. A fairly common item. Length: 4·8425in (123mm).

18 Atlantean Bus, "Esso Safety Grip tyres" by Dinky Toys; DT No 291. As (15-17), but with unplated wheels and a special finish.

1 Plymouth Yellow Cab by Dinky Toys, Great Britain; Dinky Toys Reference Number (DT No) 278, issued in 1970 and in production until 1980. Using the same casting as the Plymouth Fury Police Car (DT No 244, 1978-79), this appeared in yellow only. It has clear plastic windows, a detailed interior and a plastic whip aerial. It has a plastic chassis and is fitted with plastic speedwheels. Common. Length: 5·276in (134mm).

2 Renault Prairie by CIJ, France; dating from the 1950s. This is a simple one-piece casting and is fitted with white rubber tyres. Length: 3·937in (100mm).

3 Peugeot 404 Taxi by Dinky Toys, France; French Dinky Toys Reference Number (FDT No) 1400, dating from the 1960s. This

model features jewelled headlights, front and rear numberplates, and a detailed interior with steering wheel (left-hand drive). It is a limited item. Length: 3·976in (101mm).

4-5 Taxi with Driver; DT No 36g, first issued in 1948, in production until 1940, and reissued in 1946-49. Appearing as a separate item in the "36 Series" (ie, it was never available as part of a boxed set) this model was made in a variety of colours: the wings, top and interior were always black, but the remainder was finished in green (4), brown (5), blue, yellow, red, grey or fawn. It has a cast "Taxi" sign on the roof and a licence plate at the rear. Pre-War versions have an open rear window and are fitted with smooth wheel hubs; post-War versions are without the rear

window and have ridged wheel hubs. Both versions are limited. Length: 2·835in (72mm).

6 London Taxi Cab by Budgie Toys, Great Britain; dating from the 1960s. This model features a cast "Taxi" sign on the roof, clear plastic windows, plated wheel hubs and rubber tyres. It is a limited item. Length: 4·21in (107mm).

7-8 Austin Taxi; DT No 40h, issued in November 1951, renumbered 254 in 1955, and in production until 1962. This was the only "40 Series" vehicle to have a diecast base, which bears the maker's name, "40H" (on some earlier models) or "254" (after 1955), and "Austin taxi". It has a cast "Taxi" sign on the roof, a taxi meter, numberplates and a steering wheel. The earlier version appeared in blue or yellow

(7); in 1954-56 it was made in dark blue (8) or yellow; in 1956-62 it appeared in green-and-yellow. The earlier version is now limited. Length: 3·70in (94mm).

9 Simca 9 Aronde Taxi by Dinky Toys, France; FDT No 24ut, dating from the mid-1950s. It has a cast "Taxi" sign on the roof and a taxi meter on the bonnet and is fitted with white rubber tyres. A limited item. Length: 3·74in (95mm).

10 Ford Vedette Taxi; FDT No 24xt, dating from 1954-56. Contemporary with (9), this is also based on a car casting (FDT No 24x), with a two-tone finish applied and a sign and meter added. It is a limited item. Length: 4·134in (105mm).

11 Simca Ariane Taxi; FDT No 24zt, dating from the late 1950s. This model is fitted with clear plastic

windows and, like (10), has chromed wheel hubs. Limited. Length: 3·976in (101mm).

12 Opel Rekord Taxi; FDT No 546, dating from the early 1960s. This model, with a cast "Taxi" sign on the roof but no meter, is fitted with clear plastic windows and has a detailed interior complete with steering wheel (left-hand drive). Note the bright "Rekord" lettering on the rear wing. A limited item. Length: 4·134in (105mm).

13 Citroën ID 19 Ambulance; FDT No 556, dating from the mid-1960s. It has a plastic warning light on the roof, a cast roof rack, clear plastic windows, an opening tailgate and a detailed interior. It has "Ambulance Municipale" decals on the front doors. Length: 4·21in (107mm).

14 Renault Prairie Ambulance by CIJ,

France; dating from the 1950s. This simple model makes use of the same casting as (2), but in white finish with filled-in rear side windows, an "Ambulance" decal, and a fabric flag on a chromed staff on the right front wing. Limited. Length: 3·937in (100mm).

15 Renault Ambulance by CIJ, France; dating from the 1950s. This model, with "Ambulance" and red cross decals, has opening rear doors. Limited. Length: 4·21in (107mm).

16 Mercedes Ambulance by Lesney, Great Britain; dating from around 1969. This has opening doors and a detailed interior (left-hand drive). A fairly common model. Length: 4·134in (105mm).

17-18 Daimler Ambulance; DT No 30h. This model was first issued in 1950, appearing as shown at (17),

in cream (later in white) with red crosses, until 1954. It was renumbered 253 in March 1954 and thereafter was in production in cream or white until 1964; later production items, like the example at (18), have clear plastic windows. The tinplate base plate of the earlier version is stamped with the maker's name and "Daimler"; the number "253" is found on some later examples. In 1956 a version in matt green was issued for sale in the USA, where it was marketed as the Army Ambulance (DT No 30hm; later renumbered 624). The earlier version of this long-lived model will be the harder to find. Length: 3·78in (96mm).

19 Vauxhall Victor Ambulance; DT No 278, issued in 1964 and in production until 1968. The casting

for the Vauxhall Victor Estate Car (DT No 141, 1963-67), with the addition of a roof piece incorporating a sign and warning light, was used for this model. It is a fairly common item. Length: 3·425in (87mm).

20 Graham Paige Ambulance by Tootsietoy, USA; dating from the 1930s. This early diecast model has been repainted. It is limited. Length: 3·82in (97mm).

21 Superior Criterion Ambulance; DT No 263, issued in 1962 and in production until 1968. This model features the figures of a driver and nurse, roof-mounted warning lights, opening doors and tailgate, and a detailed interior with the figure of a patient on a stretcher. This model will be fairly easy to find. Length: 5·0in (127mm).

1 Plymouth Fury Police Car by Dinky Toys, Great Britain; Dinky Toys Reference Number (DT No) 244, issued in 1977 and in production until 1980. Like almost all Dinky Toys police vehicles, this was based on a car casting, in this case the Plymouth Stock Car (DT No 201), with the appropriate additions – warning lights, etc – decals and finish. This model has battery-powered flashing lights and a plastic whip aerial; it is fitted with a plastic chassis and plastic wheels. This model will be easy to find. Length: 5·276in (134mm).

2 Chevrolet State Police Car by Corgi Toys, Great Britain; maker's reference number (MRN) 223, issued in 1959 and in production until 1961. This model has a detailed interior (left-hand drive)

and suspension. Common. Length: 4·252in (108mm).

3 U.S.A. Police Car; DT No 258. This model appeared in four different forms between 1960 and 1968. The example shown is that available in 1960-61, based on the De Soto Fireflight (DT No 192, 1958-63). It is fitted with a flashing roof-light. The second version, based on the Dodge Royal Sedan (DT No 191, 1959-64), was available 1961-62. The third version, based on the Ford Fairlane (DT No 148, 1962-65), was available 1960-66. The fourth version, sold as the Cadillac U.S.A. Police Car, was based on the Cadillac 62 (DT No 147, 1962-68) and was available 1966-68. All four versions have black finish with white doors. The first two versions,

although not scarce, will be harder to find. Length: 4·488in (114mm).

4 Oldsmobile Sheriff's Car by Corgi; MRN 237, issued in 1962 and in production until 1966. The model bears "County Sheriff" and badge decals and is fitted with suspension. A common model. Length: 4·252in (108mm).

5 Cadillac R.C.M.P. Car; DT No 264, issued in 1966 and in production until 1968. This model, with Royal Canadian Mounted Police badge decals and with two uniformed "Mounties" inside, is based on the Cadillac 62 (DT No 147) and features a flashing light, suspension and fingertip steering. Two other models appeared with the same number: R.C.M.P. Patrol Car, 1962-66, based on the Ford Fairlane (DT No 148); Rover 3500

Police Car, (DT No 180). Fairly common. Length: 4·37in (111mm).

6 Triumph 2000 Police Car; DT No 135. This model was first issued in non-police finish in November 1963 and was in production until 1968. It has an opening bonnet with detailed engine, opening doors and boot, suspension and fingertip steering. Common. Length: 4·21in (107mm).

7 Riley Police Car by Corgi; MRN 209, issued in 1958 and in production until 1961. Finished in black-and-silver, this model has a metal "Police" sign, spotlight and bell on its roof. It is fairly common. Length: 3·819in (97mm).

8 Ford Zephyr Motorway Patrol by Corgi; MRN 419, issued in 1960 and in production until 1963. The casting incorporates a roof rack. Fairly

common. Length: 3·819in (97mm).

9 Humber Hawk Police Car; DT No 256, issued in December 1960 and in production until 1964. Based on the Humber Hawk (DT No 165, 1959-63), this model was marketed with the figures of a police driver and passenger (driver only is shown) and with the number-plate "PC 49" (the title of a then-popular radio series). It has an aerial and a roof-mounted "Police" sign and is fitted with suspension. It is one of the less common Dinky Toys police vehicles. Length: 4·016in (102mm).

10 Renault 300KG Police Radio Van by CIJ, France; dating from 1952. Note aerial with metal spring fitting. Length: 3·268in (83mm).

11 Peugeot 404 Police Car by Dinky Toys, France; French Dinky Toys

Reference Number (FDT No) 1429. This model is based on the Peugeot 404 Saloon (FDT No 553) which, in civilian finish, was marketed in Great Britain in 1962-63. It is a fairly common item. Length: 4·134in (105mm).

12 Simca 1100 Police Car by Dinky Toys, France; FDT No 1450, dating from the 1960s. A limited item. Length: 3·5625in (90mm).

13 Citroën DS 19 Police Car by Dinky Toys, France; FDT No 530, issued in 1964. This model, which has jewelled headlights, is based on the civilian-finish Citroën DS 19 with the same reference number, which was marketed in Great Britain in 1965-66. It is a limited item. Length: 4·252in (108mm).

14 Volkswagen Police Car by Corgi Toys; MRN 492, issued in 1966 and

in production until 1969. Finished in green-and-white with "Polizei" decals it has jewelled headlights. Fairly common. Length: 3·583in (91mm).

15 Renault 4CV Police Car by CIJ, France; dating from the 1960s. Note the cut-away doors on this small and simple model. A limited item. Length: 3·15in (80mm).

16 Ford Taunus Police Car; FDT No 559, dating from the later 1960s. Limited. Length: 4·055in (103mm).

17 Citroën 1200KG Police Van; FDT No 566, in production from 1965 until 1970. Note the well-modelled radiator, sliding side door and plastic "mesh" windows. Limited. Length: 4·606in (117mm).

18 Police Motor Cyclist; DT No 37b, first issued in June 1938 and in production until 1940, reissued in 1946 and available until 1948.

It is of limited availability. Length: 1·772in (45mm).

19-20 Police Motor Cycle Patrol; DT No 42b, first issued in August 1936 and in production until 1940, re-issued in 1948 and available until 1955. A limited model. Length: 1·85in (47mm).

21 Point Duty Policeman (in White Coat); DT No 42c, issued in August 1936 and available until 1941. Common. Height: 1·654in (42mm).

22 Point Duty Policeman; DT No 42d, issued in August 1936 and available until 1941. It is a common item. Height: 1·575in (40mm).

23 Police Box; DT No 42a, issued in August 1936 and in production until 1940, reissued after World War II, renumbered 751, and available until 1960. It is a common model. Height: 2·598in (66mm).

Diecast Police Vehicles by European Makers, 1960s-1980s

1 Fiat 131 "Carabinieri" Car by Urango, Italy; maker's reference number (MRN) 0140, dating from the late 1970s. Made to a scale of 1:24, this large model of an Italian police car is finished in black with a white roof, with appropriate decals. It is well detailed, with a radio aerial and spotlight of plated metal and a blue plastic warning light mounted on the roof. The bonnet opens to show a detailed engine with plated parts; the doors open on to a detailed interior of moulded plastic, with folding seats and a plated steering wheel (left-hand drive). Clear plastic windows and plastic-lensed rearlights are fitted, and it has an opening boot. The wheels and base are plastic. It is a fairly common model. Length: 6·875in (175mm).

2 Porsche 924 "Polizei" Car by Norev, France; dating around 1975. This model of a German police car, finished in black and white with appropriate markings, features a tinted plastic windscreen that incorporates details of wiper and mirror; a roof-mounted radio aerial and warning light; and an opening hatchback of tinted plastic. Length: 3·898in (99mm).

3 Simca 1100 Police Car by Dinky Toys, France (but, in fact made in Spain); French Dinky Toys No 1450, dating from 1977-1978. Finished in black and white, this model has an opening bonnet and boot, a detailed interior, clear plastic windows all round, and a roof-mounted warning light. It has a plastic base and suspension is fitted. Length: 3·583in (91mm).

4 Jaguar XJ 4·2 Police Car by Polistil, Italy; dating from the late 1970s. Made to a scale of 1:24, and finished in white with a red boot and a blue-and-red stripe, this has plated spotlights and radio aerial on the roof, together with a "Police" sign and warning light; a bonnet that opens to show a detailed engine with plated parts; doors opening on to a detailed interior with folding seats; and an opening boot on which is mounted a "Police/Stop" sign. Note the bright metal wipers on the clear plastic windscreen. Length: 7·1in (180mm).

5 Range Rover Police Vehicle by Corgi Toys, Great Britain; MRN 461, first issued in 1971 and in production until 1979. Finished in white with a red-and-blue stripe, this model features roof-mounted spotlights in plated frames and a blue plastic warning light. Clear plastic windows are fitted; the side windows slide down. The tailgate opens and plastic whizzwheels are fitted. It was sold, as shown, with a pack containing a policeman, three warning signs and nine plastic bollards. It is a common item. Length: 4·252in (108mm).

6 Rover 3500 Police Car by Corgi; MRN C339, first issued in 1980 and currently available. Finished in white with a red stripe and a badge, this has an opening bonnet and doors, and an opening hatchback with a clear plastic window that is ridged to suggest a heated screen. It is fitted with whizzwheels. Common. Length: 5·512in (140mm).

7 Police Mini Van by Corgi; MRN 448, first issued in 1964 and in

production until 1969. Finished in blue, this has jewelled headlights, clear plastic windows (the side windows permanently part-open), and rear doors that open on to an interior divided by a plastic screen across its width. The tyres are rubber. This model was sold complete with the figures of a policeman and police dog (not shown). Limited. Length: 3·11in (79mm).

8 Police Range Rover by Dinky Toys, Great Britain; Dinky Toys Number (DT No) 254, first issued in 1977 and in production until 1979. Finished in white with a blue-and-red stripe, this has jewelled headlights; a bonnet that opens to show a detailed, plated engine; and opening doors and tailgate. It is a fairly common model. Length: 4·291in (109mm).

9 Range Rover Ambulance by Corgi; MRN 482, first issued in 1974 and in production until 1977. Finished in white, the model has two blue plastic warning lights on its roof. The tailgate opens on to a detailed plastic interior. The model was sold complete with the figures of two policemen with a stretcher (not shown). Plastic whizzwheels are fitted. It is a common item. Length: 3·937in (100mm).

10 Ford Transit Police Accident Vehicle by Dinky Toys, Great Britain; DT No 287, first issued in 1967 and in production until 1974. Finished in cream with an orange stripe, this has numberplates at front and rear; jewelled headlights; a "Ford" radiator; a sliding door on the driver's side and an opening mid-door on the near side;

opening rear doors; and a roof-mounted warning light and siren. Fairly common. Length: 4·803in (122mm).

11 Ford Cortina Police Car by Corgi; MRN 402; first issued in 1974 and in production until 1977. Finished in white with orange-and-black stripes, this has a siren on the front bumper; jewelled double headlights; and doors that open on to a detailed interior with folding seats. Plastic whizzwheels are fitted. It is a fairly common item. Length: 4·016in (102mm).

12 Sunbeam Imp Panda Car by Corgi; MRN 506, first issued in 1968 and in production until 1971. Finished in blue and white, this has "Police" numberplates at front and rear; jewelled headlights; a detailed interior and an opening boot. It is

fitted with rubber tyres and incorporates "fingertip steering". The base is diecast. Fairly common. Length: 3·268in (83mm).

13 Ford Escort 1·3GL Police Car by Corgi; MRN C334, first issued in 1981 and currently available. Finished in dark blue and white (and also available in non-Police finish, in blue or red), it has a roof-mounted warning light; doors that open on to a detailed interior with tilting seats; and windscreen incorporating details of wiper and mirror. It is fitted with whizzwheels and features suspension. Common. Length: 4·409in (112mm).

Inset (above): *Police Land Rover by Britains, Great Britain; dating from the 1970s. It is fairly common. Length: 4·45in (113mm).*

Diecast Vehicles by British and French Makers, 1930s-1980s

1 E.R.F. Fire Tender by Dinky Toys, Great Britain; Dinky Toys Reference Number (DT No) 266, issued in 1976 and in production until 1980. This well-detailed model, with "Fire Service" and crest decals, is fitted with roof-mounted warning lights and bright plated hose drums, clear plastic windows and a detailed interior with steering wheel. It has a well-modelled radiator with an "ERF" logo and is fitted with treaded plastic wheels. The wheeled extending escape ladder, in white plastic, is removable. This model will be easy to find. Length overall: 8·779in (223mm).

2 E.R.F. Airport Fire Rescue Tender; DT No 263, issued in 1978 and in production until 1980. The body casting is the same as that of the E.R.F. Fire Tender at (1), but it is

finished in yellow, with "Airport Rescue" decals on the sides, "Rescue" above the cab and a crest on the doors. It is fitted with a non-extending plastic ladder. Common. Length overall: 6·969in (177mm).

3-4 Turntable Fire Escape; DT No 956, issued in February 1958 and in production until 1973. This handsome model appeared in two forms, the earlier of which is shown at (10). The two examples here are of the type appearing in 1969-73, normally in red-and-silver (4), sometimes in red-and-black, and with minor variations in finish, as at (3). Both have a large Berliet cab (note the marque name on the bright strip above the radiator) with clear plastic windows and a detailed interior. The turntable-mounted ladder, elevated and

extended by crank-handles on its mounting, is common to all versions. The later versions shown here are fairly common models. Length: 7·874in (200mm).

5 Merryweather Marquis Fire Tender; DT No 285, issued in 1969 and in production until 1980. This model, with the same decals as (1), is notable for its operating water pump: a reservoir within the toy is filled via the hatch at the right side of the roof and a press-button pump-action (the button can be seen just in front of the filler-hatch) forces water through the black hose. The three-piece plastic ladder on the roof is removable. The cab is fitted with clear plastic windows and has a detailed interior. It is a fairly common item. Length: 6·969in (177mm).

6-7 Fire Engine with Extending Ladder; DT No 555. This model was first issued by Dinky Supertoys in December 1952, was renumbered 955 in late 1954, and remained in production until 1969. Of the two examples shown, (7) is the earlier version, without plastic windows and fitted with metal wheels with rubber tyres. The example at (6) dates from after renumbering: it has windows and is fitted with plastic wheels. All versions feature a bell, a ladder that can be raised and extended, and a towing-hook. The tinplate base plate is stamped with the maker's name, "555" ("955" later) and "Fire engine". The earlier version is the harder to find. Length: 5·512in (140mm).

8 Fire Engine; DT No 259, issued in November 1961 and in production

until 1969. A Bedford vehicle, with "Fire Brigade" and crest decals on its rear sides, this model is fitted with a bell, a non-detachable ladder and clear plastic windows. It has metal wheels with rubber tyres and a tinplate base plate stamped with the maker's name and "Fire engine". It is fairly common. Length: 4·606in (117mm).

9 Airport Fire Tender; DT No 276, issued in August 1962 and in production until 1969. Another Bedford vehicle, with "Airport Fire Control" decals on its rear sides, it features a bell, a battery-powered flashing light and a rotating foam extinguisher in grey plastic. It has metal wheels with rubber tyres. Like (8), it is fitted with suspension and fingertip steering. Fairly common. Length: 4·606in (117mm).

10 Turntable Fire Escape; DT No 956; see also (3-4). This is the earlier version of the model, made in 1958-69, with a small Bedford S-Type cab and with a differently-cast rear body. It is fitted with a bell to the right of the cab roof, but the ladder and mounting are the same as on (3-4). This earlier version will be harder to find than later ones. Length: 7·874in (200mm).

11 Berliet 770 KE Camiva Fire Engine by Solido, France; maker's reference number (MRN) 352, dating from the 1970s. Length: 6·496in (165mm).

12 Berliet GBC 34 Fire Engine by Solido, France; MRN 351, dating from the 1970s. It has "Aeroport de Paris" decals and features a bright-plated swivelling foam extinguisher. Length: 5·709in (145mm).

13 Berliet Camiva 4x4 Fire Tender and Motor Pump by Solido, France; MRN 354; dating from the 1970s. Length overall: 5·827in (148mm).

14-15 Savien SG4 Fire Engine by Solido, France; dating from the 1970s. The example at (14) has "Sapeur Pompier" and crest decals and is fitted with plastic wheels; (15) lacks decals and is fitted with metal wheels with rubber tyres. Length: 4·528in (115mm).

16 Hotchkiss H6 G54 Fire Tender by Solido, France; dating from the 1970s. Length: 4·409in (112mm).

17 Citroën C35 V.S.A.B. Fire Truck with Trailer by Solido, France; MRN (truck) 368, (trailer) 371; 1970s. Length overall: 7·677in (195mm).

18-19 Streamline Fire Engine; DT No 25h, first issued in April 1936 and in production until 1940, reisssued

in 1948, renumbered 250 in 1954, and finally deleted in 1962. The example at (18) is the pre-War version, a single-piece casting with no base plate, fitted with white rubber tyres; the post-War version (19) utilises the same casting but has a tinplate base plate. The pre-War version is scarce; the post-War version is fairly common. Length: 3·976in (101mm).

20 Dodge 6x6 Fire Truck with Motor Pump by Solido, France; 1970s. Length overall: 6·693in (170mm).

21 Renault 4 Fourgonnette Fire Department Van by Solido, France; MRN 1325, dating from the 1970s. Length: 3·5625in (90mm).

22 Citroën 2CV Fire Department Van by Dinky Toys, France; FDT No 25d, dating from the 1950s. A limited item. Length: 3·307in (84mm).

1 Johnston Road Sweeper by Dinky Toys; Great Britain; Dinky Toys Reference Number (DT No) 451, issued in 1971, renumbered 449 in 1977, and in production until 1980. This model features brushes that revolve as it is pushed along; the hose is black plastic. The earliest version, issued in 1971, has opening doors: this will be harder to find than later examples, as shown, with non-opening doors. It is fairly common. Length: 5·591in (142mm).

2-3 Snow Plough; DT No 958, issued in January 1961 and in production until 1965. This Supertoys model uses the Guy Warrior chassis and is fitted with a blade that lifts back over the cab. It appeared only in yellow-and-black but, as shown, with variations in the colour of the blade.

Limited. Length overall: 7·677in (195mm). Shown just to the right and in front of (3) is the Breakdown Jeep; FDT No 1412, issued in 1968 and in production until 1971. Length: 3·307in (84mm).

4 Mercedes Snow Plough by Dinky Toys, France; French Dinky Toys Reference Number (FDT No) 567, issued in 1967 and in production until 1970. It features an adjustable blade and a black plastic canopy. Length overall: 5·709in (145mm).

5 Snow Plough with Trailer by Solido, France; maker's reference number 213, dating from the 1970s. It is fitted with plastic wheels. Length overall: 8·189in (208mm).

6 Ford D800 Snow Plough/Tipper; DT No 439, issued in 1970 and in production until 1976. With an adjustable blade and a tipping

back, this model appeared in several finishes, but with the blade always in yellow. The cab has clear plastic windows and opening doors. Fairly common. Length overall: 7·638in (194mm).

7 LMV Road Sweeper; FDT No 596, issued in 1960 and in production until 1963. It is fitted with a brush that revolves and pivots as the vehicle moves. Length: 4·882in (124mm).

8-9 Refuse Wagon; DT No 978, issued in 1964 and in production until 1979. Using the Bedford TK cab and chassis, this appeared in various colours and features a rear body (plastic) that tips forward and back, with opening rear doors. It may be found with or without opening doors to the cab, and with a roof box either of plastic (earlier) or cast (1978-79). Note also the wheel variation in

the two examples shown. Common. Length: 5·984in (152mm).

10-11 Citroën U23 Breakdown Truck; FDT No 35A, issued in 1955, renumbered 582, and in production until 1971. Of the examples shown, (11) has a metal hook and dates from before 1959; (10) has a plastic hook. In both cases, the crane is tinplate and "Dinky Service" is stamped in yellow. Length: 4·921in (125mm).

12 Berliet GAK Breakdown Truck; FDT No 589, issued in 1965 and in production until 1969. It has a plastic aerial and roof-mounted warning light. Length: 4·803in (122mm).

13-14 Bedford TK Crash Truck; DT No 434, issued in April 1964 and in production until 1972. This model is fitted with an operating winch. The version at (14), in green-and-

white with "Top Rank" decals, is the more common; the red-black-and-white "Auto Services" version (13) appeared only for a short time. Length: 4·803in (122mm).

15-17 Commer Breakdown Lorry; originally issued as DT No 25x in September 1950, renumbered 430 in 1954, and in production until 1963. Fitted with an operating winch and a towing-hook, and with "Dinky Service" decals, this model appeared first in brown-and-green and thereafter in other finishes. The example at (15) is a late one, with windows. Fairly common. Length: 4·843in (123mm).

18-20 Bedford Refuse Wagon; DT No 25v, issued in October 1948, renumbered 252 in 1954, and in production until 1964. It has a tipping body with sliding doors. It

was first issued as seen at (19), in fawn-and-green and without windows. The versions at (18) and (20)—note wheel variations—date from after 1954. Fairly common. Length: 4·21in (107mm).

21 R.A.C. Patrol Van; DT No 273, issued in 1965 and in production until 1969. This Mini-Van is fitted with a peg-in plastic roof sign. Common. Length: 3·071in (78mm).

22 R.A.C. Guide at the Salute; DT No 43d, issued in October 1935 and in production until 1940. A common item. Height: 1·417in (36mm).

23-24 R.A.C. Motor Cycle Patrol; DT No 43b, issued in October 1935 and in production until 1940, and reissued in 1948-49. The pre-War version (23) is fitted with white solid rubber wheels and has a driver with a well-detailed uniform; the

post-War version (24) has black solid rubber wheels. The pre-War version is limited; the post-War version is fairly common. Lengths: (pre-War) 1·811in (46mm); (post-War) 1·772in (45mm).

25 R.A.C. Box; DT No 43a, issued in October 1935 and in production until 1940. Lithographed tinplate. Limited. Height: 2·008in (51mm).

26 R.A.C. Guide Directing Traffic; DT No 43c, issued in October 1935 and in production until 1940. Common. Height: 1·457in (37mm).

27 A.A. Box; DT No 44a, issued in October 1935 and in production until 1940. It is of lithographed tinplate, with three tinplate signs. Limited. Length: 3·189in (81mm).

28-30 A.A. Motor Cycle Patrol; DT No 44b, issued in October 1935 and in production until 1940; reissued

in 1946, renumbered 270, and in production until 1963. At (28) is a post-War model, with solid black rubber wheels. (Note that post-renumbering versions have grey plastic wheels.) At (29-30) are pre-War versions, with solid white rubber wheels. Fairly common. Length: 1·811in (46mm).

31 A.A. Guide Saluting; DT No 44d, issued in October 1935 and in production until 1940. A common item. Height: 1·417in (36mm).

32 A.A. Guide Directing Traffic; DT No 44c, issued in October 1935 and in production until 1940. Common. Height: 1·457in (37mm).

33 A.A. Patrol Van; DT No 274, issued in 1964 and in production until 1972. Except for its finish, this is the same model as (21). A common item. Length: 3·071in (78mm).

1 Atlas Digger by Dinky Toys, Great Britain; Dinky Toys Reference Number (DT No) 984, issued in 1974 and in production until 1979. (Note that the same reference number was used for the Car Transporter of 1958-63, shown at (5), pages 72-73). Appearing only in the finish shown, this large model features clear plastic windows, a detailed cab and a manually-operated working shovel action. The shovel unit swivels on a turntable mounted on a base that is fitted with black plastic caterpillar tracks. Since models of construction plant, like this and other items on this spread, invited "active play", they may be harder to find in good condition than other Dinky Toys models of this relatively late period. This model, however, is common.

Length overall: 9·724in (247mm).
2 Albion Lorry-Mounted Concrete Mixer; DT No 960, issued in August 1960 and in production until 1967. Appearing only in orange-yellow-and-blue finish, this Dinky Supertoys model features a cement hopper that rotates as the vehicle moves and can be manually tipped. The cab is fitted with clear plastic windows; note the centre-mounted spare wheel on the body. It is fitted with six wheels (double wheels at rear) with the typical Supertoys tyres of grey rubber. It is a fairly common item. Length: 5·039in (128mm).
3 Elevator Loader; DT No 564, first issued in November 1952, re-numbered 964 in 1954-55, and in production until 1968. This was originally issued as a Dinky

Supertoys model and was intended to complement Gauge "0" toy railway layouts; it has, however, come to be classified with the Farm and Garden range of models. The loading ramp (originally fitted with a detachable tailgate that is missing from this example) is lifted by the lever visible on the far side of the vehicle; the load – sand, gravel, or the like – is then raised on the endless black rubber tracks to pour down the chute into a waiting truck. Note the cast detail on the model's exterior. Fairly common. Length overall: 6·142in (156mm).
4 Foden Dump Truck with Bulldozer Blade; DT No 959, issued in October 1961 and in production until 1968. Fitted with clear plastic windows and with the figure of a driver in the cab, this Supertoys

model has a tipping rear body and a blade that can be raised and lowered. A fairly common model. Length overall: 6·654in (169mm).
5 Aveling-Barford Centaur Dump Truck; DT No 924, issued in 1972 and in production until 1976. Appearing only with a red cab and yellow tipping rear body (note the control handle to the rear of the cab), this model is fitted with clear plastic windows, a detailed cab, and black plastic tyres. Common. Length: 7·087in (180mm).
6 Michigan 180 Tractor-Dozer; DT No 976, issued in 1968 and in production until 1976. Appearing only in yellow-and-red, this model (which was marketed in a bubble-pack) features a detachable cab with the figure of a driver, a removable engine cover, and a

blade that can be raised and lowered. It has black plastic tyres. A common item. Length overall: 5·787in (147mm).

7 Road Grader; DT No 963, issued in 1973 and in production until 1976. Like (6), this irregularly-shaped model, with a movable blade and steerable rear wheels, was marketed in a bubble-pack. A common item. Length overall: 9·37in (238mm).

8 Shovel Dozer; DT No 977, issued in 1973 and in production until 1978. Another awkwardly-shaped model that was marketed in a bubble-pack, this is fitted with clear plastic windows, a movable blade and plastic crawler tracks. Common. Length overall: 5·945in (151mm).

9 Marrel Multi-Bucket Unit; DT No 966, issued in December 1960 and in production until 1964.

Making use of the same Albion cab as the Lorry-Mounted Concrete Mixer shown at (2), this Dinky Supertoys model of a skip lorry is fitted with clear plastic windows and has a working skip. It appeared only in yellow finish with a grey skip, as shown. It is fairly common. Length: 4·528in (115mm).

10 Eaton Yale Articulated Tractor Shovel; DT No 973, issued in 1971 and in production until 1976. Another large and unwieldy model that was marketed in a bubble-pack, this is fitted with clear plastic windows, a detailed cab and a movable shovel. It bears "Yale 6000" and "F.T.N." decals at the rear. It is a quite common item. Length overall: 7·008in (178mm).

11 Terex Rear Dump Truck; DT No 965, issued in 1969 and in

production until 1970. This model is basically the same casting as (12) and (13) and bears the same number; however, it embodies minor changes to the casting of cab and base plate (on which "Euclid" was altered to "Terex") necessitated when the name of the "sponsor" company was changed in 1969. Like all post-1963 models in the Road-Making Equipment range, it is fitted with clear plastic windows. For further details of the model, see (12). It is a fairly common item. Length: 5·591in (142mm).

12 Euclid Rear Dump Truck; DT No 965, issued in October 1955 and in production until 1956. This is the original version of DT No 965, marked as such by its lack of windows, the green motif on its badge decal, and its rubber tyres

with a less-marked tread than those of the later versions seen at (11) and (13). Its tipping rear is activated by the crank-handle visible just below and to the rear of the cab. Its diecast base bears the maker's name, "Euclid rear dump truck" and "965". Length: 5·591in (142mm).

13 Euclid Rear Dump Truck; DT No 965. This is the form in which the model described at (12) appeared in 1956-59, until it was replaced by the "Terex" version shown at (11). It differs from (12) in having the motif of the badge (a sticker rather than a decal may be found on some examples) in red-and-black, in the provision of clear plastic windows, and in the more pronounced tread of its tyres. Length: 5·591in (142mm).

1 Coles 20-Ton Lorry-Mounted Crane by Dinky Toys, Great Britain; Dinky Toys Reference Number (DT No) 972, issued in May 1955 and in production until 1968. Appearing only in orange-and-yellow, this Supertoys model features the cast figures of drivers in both lorry and crane cabs. The crane body swivels, and the hook is raised or lowered by the crank-handle on the side of the body; the angle of the jib is adjusted by a similar handle on the other side — see (2). It is fitted with six wheels with black rubber tyres and has a tinplate base plate. This is a fairly common item. Length overall: 9·449in (240mm).

2 Coles 20-Ton Lorry-Mounted Crane by Dinky Toys, France; French Dinky Toys Reference Number (FDT No) 972, issued in 1957, renumbered

889, again renumbered 972L, and in production until 1958. The same casting as the British model (1), but with grey rubber tyres.

3 Jones Fleetmaster Cantilever Crane; DT No 970, issued in 1967 and in production until 1976. With a working crane operated by a crank-handle, this model first appeared in red-white-and-yellow, and then, as shown, in metallic red and white. This is a fairly common model. Length overall: 6·85in (174mm).

4 Goods Yard Crane; DT No 752, issued in February 1953, re-numbered 973 in January 1955, and in production until 1959. An interesting and unusual model in that it is not fitted with wheels, this was announced as being for use with Gauge "0" toy-railways. An all-diecast model, it has working

crane action with an adjustable jib, controlled by crank-handles on either side. It is fairly common. Length of base: 3·937in (100mm); (height) 7·677in (195mm).

5 Salev Mobile Crane; FDT No 50, issued in April 1957, renumbered 595, and in production until 1959. It has a working crane controlled by crank-handles and is complete with driver. Length: 6·142in (156mm).

6-7 Coles Mobile Crane; DT No 571, issued in December 1949, re-numbered 971 in 1954-55, and in production until 1965. This Supertoys model has a swivelling body and a fully-operating crane controlled by a crank-handle. At (6) is an earlier version, with grey rubber tyres and a brass handle to its crank; (7) has black tyres and a plastic handle. Fairly common.

Length overall: 6·299in (160mm).

8 Berliet GBO Saharien; FDT No 888, issued in 1960, in production until 1966, and briefly reissued in 1968. This model of an oil exploration vehicle has a block-and-tackle operated by a crank-handle. Earlier examples have diecast wheels; later ones will be found with plastic wheels fitted. Length: 6·732in (171mm).

9 Richier Road Scraper; FDT No 886, issued in 1960 and in production until 1965. Fitted with a fairly complex and rather unsatisfactory control system for its swivelling blade, this model has a diecast driver. Length: 6·929in (176mm).

10 Servicing Platform Vehicle; DT No 977, issued in September 1960 and in production until 1964. Parallel wires on either side

support the elevatable platform; the stays on either side may be folded up or down. Common. Length overall: 7·756in (197mm).

11-12 Blaw-Knox Bulldozer; DT No 561, issued in January 1949, renumbered 961 in 1955, and in production until 1964. It has a driver and is equipped with a lifting blade and rubber caterpillar tracks. The example at (11) is the earlier version, which appeared in red only. At (12) is a post-renumbering version in yellow with a grey blade; the model also appeared for a short time in green-and-orange plastic. Fairly common. Length overall: 5·433in (138mm).

13 Blaw-Knox Bulldozer; FDT No 885, issued in October 1959 and in production unti 1961. This resembles the British model (11-12)

in all respects, save that its tinplate base plate is stamped *"Assemblé en France"*. Length: as (11-12).

14 Blaw-Knox Heavy Tractor; DT No 563, issued in August 1948, renumbered 963 in January 1955, and in production until 1959. This is the same casting as the Bulldozer (11-12), minus the blade. Common. Length: 4·567in (116mm).

15 G.M.C. 6x6 Truck by FJ, France; dating from the 1960s. This model is fitted with an adjustable shovel and has a tipping rear. Limited. Length: 5·315in (135mm).

16 Berliet GBO Quarry Truck; FDT No 572, issued in 1970 and in production until 1971. Using the same chassis as the Berliet GBO Saharien, see (8), this model is fitted with a tipping rear body that is made of yellow plastic.

Length: 7·402in (188mm).

17 Coventry-Climax Fork-Lift Truck; DT No 14c, issued in November 1949, renumbered 401 in 1954, and in production until 1964. This has a fork-lift raised by a crank-handle on its side. Fairly common. Length: 4·252in (108mm).

18 Coventry-Climax Fork-Lift Truck; FDT No 597, issued in 1959 and in production until 1961. It uses the same casting as the British model (17), but its tinplate base plate is stamped *"Assemblé en France"*.

19-20 Aveling-Barford Diesel Roller; DT No 25p, issued in February 1948, renumbered 251 in 1954, and in production until 1963. Appearing only in green-and-red but with variations in shades, this has a swivelling front roller. It is fairly common.

Length: 4·3125in (110mm).

21 Richier Diesel Roller; FDT No 90A, issued in 1958, renumbered 830 in 1959, and in production until 1969. It is fitted with a swivelling front roller. Length: 4·409in (112mm).

22 Muir-Hill Dumper Truck; DT No 562, issued in September 1948, renumbered 962 in 1954-55, and in production until 1965. Appearing only in yellow, it has a tipping rear body and is fitted with a towing-hook. A common item. Length: 4·134in (105mm).

23 Muir-Hill Dumper Truck; FDT No 887, issued in 1959 and in production until 1961. This resembles the British model (22) in all save its black rubber tyres and the words *"Assemblé en France"* stamped on its tinplate base plate. Length: 4·134in (105mm).

Diecast Farm Equipment by British Makers, 1930s–1970s

1 Farm Trailer by Britains, Great Britain; Britains Catalogue Number (BCN) 130F, dating from around 1948. The rubber-tyred trailer, fitted with detachable racks and with a tipping rear body with a hinged tailboard, is intended to be towed by a tractor. It is a common item. Length: 4·488in (114mm).

2-3 Halesowen Harvest Trailer by Dinky Toys, Great Britain; Dinky Toys Reference Number (DT No) 27b, issued in June 1949, renumbered 320 in 1954, and in production until 1970. It is fitted with removable racks, a tow-bar and a towing-hook at the rear. An early version with diecast wheels is shown at (2); at (3) is a post-renumbering example, which has plastic wheels fitted with black rubber tyres. A fairly common

model. Length: 4·764in (121mm).

4 Leyland 384 Tractor; DT No 308, issued in 1971 and in production until 1979. This model, which was marketed in a bubble-pack, is fitted with a towing-hook and is shown pulling the Halesowen Harvest Trailer, see (2-3). A common item. Length: 3·386in (86mm).

5 Massey-Ferguson Tractor; DT No 300, and Massey-Harris Spreader, DT No 321. The Tractor was first issued as the Massey-Harris Farm Tractor, DT No 27a, in June 1948; it was renumbered 300 in 1954 and remained in production until 1971. It is fitted with swivelling front wheels. The Manure Spreader was first issued as DT No 27c in October 1949; it was renumbered 321 in 1954 and remained in production until 1973. Note the

working parts at the rear, activated by a metal driveband from the axle. The example shown attached to the tractor is a post-renumbering version; to the right is an earlier version, with diecast wheels. Both models are fairly common. Lengths: (tractor) 3·504in (89mm); (spreader) 4·449in (113mm).

6 Muir-Hill 2WL Loader; DT No 437, issued in February 1962 and in production until 1980. This model has a working shovel. Common. Length: 4·134in (105mm).

7 Timber Carriage with Log; BCN 12F, dating from the 1940s. This was issued as part of a five-piece set, along with two horses and a farmhand. The log is real wood and the carriage has an adjustable chassis. A fairly common item. Length: 8in (203mm).

8 Week's Tipping Farm Trailer; DT No 319, issued in June 1961 and in production until 1970. The two-wheeled trailer is fitted with a tow-bar and has a tipping body with a hinged tailboard. A common item. Length: 4·134in (105mm).

9 Disc Harrow; BCN 135F, dating from c1948. This is a common model. Length: 2·25in (57mm).

10 Four-Furrow Tractor Plough; BCN 138F, dating from about 1948. The red-handled arms are used to adjust the angle of the plough's blades to three different positions. Common. Length: 7·008in (178mm).

11 Farm Tractor and Hay Rake; DT No 27ak. Issued in March 1953, this is a set consisting of the Massey-Harris Farm Tractor, DT No 27a, see (5), and the Hay Rake, DT No 27k. The set was renumbered 310 in 1954

and was in production until 1966. Limited. Length overall: 6·181in (157mm). Shown immediately to the right is a Roller; BCN 136F.

12-13 Field Marshall Farm Tractor; DT No 27n, issued in October 1953, renumbered 301 in 1954, and in production until 1965. It has a swivelling front axle and is fitted with a towing-hook. Limited. Length: 3·11in (79mm).

14-15 David Brown Tractor and Disc Harrow; DT No 325, issued in 1966 as a set consisting of DT No 325 (Tractor) and DT No 322 (Disc Harrow), and available in this form until 1972. At (15) the tractor is shown with its cab removed; note also the variation in colour finish. The Harrow, which has rotating discs, is also shown in two different finishes. Fairly common. Lengths: (tractor) 3·268in (83mm); (harrow) 3·386in (86mm).

16 Fordson Tractor; BCN 128F, dating from 1948. This model is marked as a later-type issue by its balloon-tyres; see also (17). It is fairly common. Length: 4in (102mm).

17 Fordson Tractor; BCN 127F, dating from the 1940s. Its "spudded" metal wheels show that this is an earlier model than that at (16). Limited. Length: 4in (102mm).

18 Farm Tractor; DT No 22e, one of the original "Modelled Miniatures" announced by Meccano in December 1933. This diminutive tractor, with a cast-in steering wheel, a towing-hook and metal wheels, is based on a Fordson. It remained in production until World War II and is now a rare model. Length: 2·756in (70mm).

19 Fordson Major Tractor; Britains "Lilliput" series, BCN 604, dating from around 1950. A limited item. Length: 1·75in (44mm).

20 Motocart; DT No 27g, issued in December 1949, renumbered 342 in 1954, and in production until 1961. It is a common item. Length: 4·3125in (110mm).

21 Land Rover (Pick Up); DT No 344, issued in 1970 and in production until 1977. It has an opening bonnet and doors. Common. Length: 4·252in (108mm).

22-23 Land Rover; DT No 27d, issued in April 1950, renumbered 340 in 1954, and in production until 1970. Note the tinplate windscreen frame and spare wheel. The model normally appeared in green-and-orange (23); in the paint finish shown at (22), it is scarce.

Length: 3·5625in (90mm).

24 Land Rover; DT No 340, with Land Rover Trailer, DT No 341. The two-wheeled trailer was first issued in 1954 as DT No 27m; it was almost immediately renumbered 341 and remained in production until 1973. Fairly common. Length: 3·11in (79mm).

25 Tumbrel Cart with Horse and Hay Racks; Britains "Lilliput" series, BCN 606, dating from c1950. Limited. Length: 2·75in (70mm).

26 Milk Float and Horse, BCN 605, with Stable Lad, BCN 531; Britains "Lilliput" series, dating from about 1950. Limited. Length (horse and cart): 2·25in (57mm).

27 Dairy Cart with Milkman and Two Churns; BCN 131F, dating from c1950. Limited. Length (horse and cart): 5in (127mm).

Tinplate Passenger Boats by German Makers, 1900s-1940s

Toy boats are among the most beautiful and desirable of all transport toys, but because they are comparatively fragile and also particularly liable to accidental loss—the lakes and ponds of the world must have bottoms carpeted with fine tinplate boats!—they are also among the scarcest and most valuable tinplate toys.

Examples in good condition, especially earlier items by makers of the "classic" period, are less often encountered than equivalent toys of other kinds. Such details as ships' boats, anchors, masts, flags and (almost invariably) rigging are often missing, and many boats will have undergone, or will need, restoration. The boats shown here, all in very good condition (some having undergone minor restoration

by a professional hand) and by noted makers, may all be described as rare or very scarce. All the boats shown on this spread are from the collection of Ron McCrindell, Sidmouth, Devon.

1 River Boat by Carette, Nuremburg, Germany; dating from around 1906. This most attractive pleasure steamer has a spirit-fired brass boiler and a single oscillating cylinder. Note particularly the operating windlass, with anchor and chain, forward, and the wheel, aft, that turns the rudder. Despite its pacific appearance, it will be noticed that the steamer's hull incorporates a pronounced "ram" bow: obviously, the same hull was used by Carette for a model warship! The seated terracotta

passengers are figures of the same period as the boat, but were made by Gebrüder Märklin of Nuremburg to complement that maker's toy trains. This steamer is fitted with American flags fore and aft; and since toy boats were normally fitted with the appropriate flags for the areas where they were to be sold, we may assume that this example was intended for the US market. Founded in Nuremburg in 1886, the toymaking firm of George Carette & Cie established an international reputation, primarily for tinplate boats and toy trains. Carette, a French citizen, was forced to leave Germany during World War I, and the firm's production ended in 1917. Although it is some 80 years old, this boat is in good working order: it was seen

proceeding under steam in the BBC2 Television film "Ron McCrindell's Toys" (1973). It has undergone some restoration, but is seen in near-original condition. Length: 19·685in (50cm).

2 Liner by Arnold, West Germany; dating from immediately after World War II. This simple tinplate model was made in five sizes. Note the shallow draft of the hull, which is less realistic than in earlier German tinplate boats: presumably it was necessary, at the time of manufacture, to economise on material and allow the toy to be marketed at the lowest possible price. The deck is secured by tab-and-slot; thus, although the boat is not designed to be disassembled, access to the clockwork mechanism may be

fairly easily gained in an emergency. The masts and flags are missing from this example, but it is otherwise in good order. Note the partly-visible Arnold trademark stamped in the bows of this model. Length: 8·75in (22·225cm).

3 Paddle Steamer by Carette, Nuremburg, Germany; this model was catalogued in 1911 but probably dates from some years earlier. It has undergone restoration to near-original condition and finish: as noted elsewhere in this book, restoration of professional standard is acceptable (and very often most necessary!) on rare boats of this vintage. However, the fore and aft masts are missing. The boat is clockwork-powered and has a winding aperture just aft of the paddlewheel on the side away from

the camera: it may be noted that this winding aperture is set so low in the hull that operation in all but the calmest waters would hazard the boat! This model was marketed in several sizes, of which the example shown here was the largest, with a length of 20·866in (53cm).

4 Liner "Viking" by Arnold, Germany; dating from the mid-1930s. At that period, this simple, clockwork-powered tinplate boat was sold in Great Britain for about 7½d (3p, 4c). Note the lithographed detail of deck fittings: this is a characteristic feature of boats by Arnold. The foremast is missing from the example of the boat shown here. Length: 7·874in (20cm).

5 Liner by Gebrüder Bing, Nuremburg, Germany; dating from around 1928. This clockwork-

powered tinplate model was marketed for a period of about three years, during which time it was made in seven different sizes, of which the largest was 39·37in (1m) long. Since this example flies the Union Jack forward and the Red Ensign aft, we may assume—see note at (1)—that it was intended for sale on the British market. Length: 19·685in (50cm).

6 Turbine Steamboat by Gebrüder Bing, Nuremburg, Germany; dating from around 1906. This is a very rare boat and of particular interest in that it is driven by a small steam turbine, with a methylated-spirit-fired boiler. Its construction, too, is notable: for the canopy, Bing used a stamping originally made for a model railway station, while the cabin aft is, in fact, a Bing Gauge

"0" railway carriage without its wheels. This model appeared in three sizes, one larger and one smaller than our example, which is 16·14in (41cm) long.

7 Liner by Arnold, Germany, a very similar model to that shown at (4) and of about the same period, but slightly larger and with some differences in the lithographed details of the deck fittings. This clockwork-powered tinplate boat is unusual in that it has its winding aperture at the stern, near the top of the hull, rather than winding through the funnel: this is a feature that the boat's present owner, a very experienced collector, has encountered only on some boats made by Arnold and Bing—and never on boats by other makers. Length: 9in (22·86cm).

All the boats shown on this spread are from the collection of Ron McCrindell, Sidmouth, Devon.

1 Liner "Luzern" by Gebrüder Märklin, Göppingen, Germany; dating from the period immediately after World War I. (It may be noted, however, that as is also the case with boats by other makers, this boat's style differs very little from that of an equivalent example dating from the pre-World War I period, or even from the 1930s.) A Märklin (Wittenburg) trademark is stamped on the side of the rudder that is turned away from the camera in this photograph. This most attractive tinplate boat, although not one of Märklin's "classic" items, is well-proportioned, interestingly-detailed (note the

"rubber-stamped" portholes on the hull), nicely finished, and in first-class original condition. It is clockwork-powered: the winding aperture can be seen just aft of the second funnel. As was a common practice with German makers in the period following both World Wars, this liner bears a Swiss name and is fitted with Swiss flags; see also (3-6). It is to be regretted that the Märklin series of which this boat formed a part had only a brief production run. Founded in the 1850s by Theodor Friedrich Wilhelm Märklin, the great toy-making firm that produced this liner traded as Gebrüder Märklin from 1880 onward, and remains an international leader in toy production to this day. It was in its earlier days particularly notable as

an innovator in the field of toy trains, exhibiting what was probably the first "train set" in the modern sense—ie, one capable of extension by the purchase of a series of further components—at the Leipzig Trade Fair of 1891. No less successful than the toy trains were the maker's toy boats: many collectors would claim—and judging from present-day auction prices, many more would agree!— that Märklin's boats are the most desirable of all. As in the case of the boats shown on *pages 108-109,* all the tinplate boats shown on this spread, which are in fine condition, are either rare or very scarce. Length: 14·2in (36cm).

2 Liner by Fleischmann, Nuremburg, Germany; dating from the 1930s. This clockwork-driven boat, based

on the maker's favoured 52cm hull, appeared in the Fleischmann catalogue for 1936, was in production until 1939, and made a brief reappearance in 1955-56. Note particularly the lifeboats: their simple design is a characteristic of the maker. The Fleischmann company, still in production but now probably best-known for its toy trains, was founded in 1887 and from the outset established its reputation with its toy boats. The firm acquired much of Georges Carette's tooling when his company ceased operations in 1917—see note at (1), *pages 108-109*—and maintained its high standards in spite of diversification into the manufacture of other mechanical toys (especially after the takeover of the Staudt company in 1928)

7

8   9   10

and, after the takeover of Doll et Cie just before World War II, into increasing specialisation in the toy trains for which it is noted. Length: 20·5in (52cm).

3-6 Set of Liners by the Arnold Company, West Germany; the boxes in which these clockwork-driven boats were sold are marked "Made in Germany, US Zone", but the models were probably made before World War II and repackaged — tactfully fitted with Swiss flags; see note at (1) — for sale after the War. With Fleischmann, the Arnold company, founded in 1906, was about the last to maintain the great German tradition of tinplate boats after World War II — until the growing dominance of plastic in the 1960s, along with the aggressive marketing tactics of the Far Eastern tinplate

toymakers rendered uneconomical the mass-production of such comparatively expensive toys. Still in production, Arnold is perhaps now best-known for its small-gauge toy railways. In the set of boats shown here, the two larger liners, (5) and (4), with three funnels and two funnels respectively, have twin propellers; the two smaller, (3) and (6), with two funnels and one funnel respectively, are each fitted with a single propeller. This set is of particular interest to the collector in that its components are among the last of the high-quality tinplate boats in the long-established German tradition that began in the latter part of the 19th century. Lengths: (5) 18·11in (46cm); (4) 14·57in (37cm); (3) 11·81in (30cm); (6) 9·055in (23cm).

7-10 Set of Liners by Fleischmann, Nuremburg, Germany; dating from the mid-1930s. It is interesting to note the influence of Georges Carette, the famous French maker who traded at Nuremburg as George (*sic*) Carette & Cie until forced to give up his business during World War I, on these clockwork-driven tinplate boats, particularly the largest (8). The masts, especially, are in the Carette style, as is the superstructure — and this is hardly surprising, since these boats were made up from Carette pressings obtained after World War I; see also note at (2), above. The simple lifeboats, however, are in the characteristic style of Fleischmann. Like the set of liners by Arnold shown at (3-6), these Fleischmann boats stand

near the end of the line of the traditional German tinplate toy boats. It should be noted, also, that although we describe these boats, and the Arnold examples at (3-6), as a "set", since they are near-identical models in graduated sizes, the boats were not intended to be marketed as a set but were sold as separate items. They were also made in other sizes than those shown here. Note the simple stands on the undersides of the boats' hulls, near the bows. Note also that these boats are in fine condition: toy boats will often be found in "play-worn" condition and will need restoration — which is best entrusted to a professional restorer. Lengths: (8) 12·99in (33cm); (9) 10·63in (27cm); (10) 8·66in (22cm); (7) 7·48in (19cm).

1 Paddle Steamer by G.G. Kellermann and Company, Nuremburg, Germany; dating from the late 1930s. This is an ingenious dual-purpose clockwork-powered toy: it operates in the normal way in water, and may also be used as a "carpet toy", when it is supported and driven by its paddle-wheels and steered by means of the third wheel fixed to the rudder. It is of pressed tin construction, with printed details of deck fittings, cabins and crew, etc, and with a tinplate flag in the bows. Note the permanently-fixed key protruding through the funnel: its winder is made in the shape of a cloud of smoke, a pleasant detail that has been a feature of the cheaper tinplate toy boats throughout the century. This toy bears on its underside the "CKO" trademark of the Kellermann company, which was founded in 1910 and remained active into the post-World War II period. Like most tinplate toy boats, this item is now of limited availability. Length: 10·75in (27·305cm).

2 Three-Funnelled Liner by Gebrüder Bing, Nuremburg, Germany; dating from the mid-1920s. This clockwork-powered liner by one of the most famous makers of tinplate toys, known worldwide for the boats, cars, railways and other toys produced in the period c1890-1934, is unusual in that it is fitted with battery-powered port and starboard recognition lights. The red-lensed port-side light and the socket (the lens is missing from this example) for the green-lensed starboard light are visible beneath the front of the lift-off superstructure, which also houses the battery compartment. This liner was also produced without lights and was marketed in several different hull-sizes. The example shown has undergone restoration: the lifeboats and flags are not original. Scarce. Length: 13·25in (33·655cm).

3 One-Funnelled Liner by an unidentified maker, possibly of West German manufacture, dating from around 1950. This bears only a "Foreign" marking, but it is similar to the tinplate boats marketed after World War II by Arnold, West Germany (although Arnold toys of the immediate post-War period normally bear the firm's name/mark and the words "Made in US Zone"). See also (4). It consists of a keel-less hull pressing and simple super-structure, with the winding-shank for its clockwork mechanism just visible within the top of the funnel. It is shown in its original finish; unrestored. This is a limited item. Length: 9·375in (23·8125cm).

4 Two-Funnelled Liner by an unidentified maker, possibly by Arnold, Germany; dating from around 1930. This neat little tinplate liner, with the winding-shank for its clockwork mechanism protruding at the stern, has a rudder of a shape characteristic of the products of the Arnold company; a similar putative attribution on stylistic ground is made in the case of the one-funnelled liner shown at (3). Note the simple wire support on the underside of the well-formed hull. With painted port-holes and

other details printed, this boat is shown in its original finish. Limited. Length: 7·00in (17·78cm).

5 "Conte Verde" Liner by Ingap (Industria Nazionale Giocattoli Automatica Padova), Padua, Italy, dating from around 1920; note the maker's diamond-enclosed trademark on the bow. This three-funnelled "carpet toy" liner, mounted on four large wheels, is of attractively-printed lightweight tinplate. It is powered by wire-spring clockwork. Limited. Length: 11·00in (27·94cm).

6 Single-Engine Monoplane by an unidentified British maker—note that "Made in England", printed along the upper rear edge of the starboard wing, is its only mark of origin—dating from just before World War II. This printed tinplate aeroplane, which bears the

registration letters "G-E OBT", has a two-piece fuselage of pressed tin, with the half-figure of a pilot in an open cockpit, and a detachable push-through wing section. A clockwork motor with a permanently-fixed winder drives the pressed-tin wheels, which are printed with spokes and "5 x 19 Balloon Tyres". A limited item. Wingspan: 14·00in (35·56cm).

7 Tri-Motor "Air France" Air Liner by Joustra (Societé d'Exploitation du Jouet Joustra), Strasbourg-Neudorf, France; dating from the late 1930s. The trademark of the wellknown maker, established in 1934 and one of the few Western toymakers to continue in production with tinplate toys into the 1970s-1980s, can be seen towards the tail. This low-wing monoplane,

bearing the registration letters "F-POU" on its fuselage sides and the legend "Air France" just forward of its cockpit, is of printed tinplate. It is interesting to compare it with the rather similar aeroplane made by a British toymaker at around the same time, shown at (6). A clockwork motor with a permanently-fixed winder drives the two large wheels on the undercarriage and, via coil springs, the propellers. The wheel mounted beneath the tail can be used to steer the toy. Limited. Wingspan: 12·875in (32·7025cm).

8 Tri-Motor Air Liner by S. Günthermann, Nuremburg, Germany; dating from around 1935. This high-wing monoplane is a later example of the work of a manufacturer established in Nuremburg in the late 19th century

—a pioneer in the production of clockwork-powered tinplate toys. It has nicely printed details of an engine on its nose, and bears the registration number "1424"—which may also be the maker's reference number—on its wings, fuselage and tailplane. Note particularly the cut-out side windows in the fuselage and the "flying hook", at the centre of gravity so that the model may be suspended and "flown" on a cord, at the centre-rear of the detachable wing section. A clockwork motor drives the wheels on the undercarriage, which are printed with details of "6 x 24 Balloon Tyres", and the large nose-mounted propeller. The smaller propellers can only be revolved manually. A limited item. Wingspan: 16·375in (41·5925cm).

1 Douglas DC-6B Airliner by Arnold, West Germany; dating from c1951 (ie, the model appeared at about the same time that the prototype entered airline service). This tinplate airliner is shown in KLM livery, with the legend "De Vliegende Hollander" along the starboard fuselage and its English equivalent, "The Flying Dutchman", to port; see also (3). The identification letters "PE-DFY" appear on the upper and lower starboard wing surfaces and on the tailplane. The model is clockwork-powered, with drive to the rubber main wheels, with a winding aperture on the port side of the nose. Small control knobs on the underside of the fuselage, between the main wheels, allow for the aircraft to be stationary with the inner propellers

turning, or moving forward with all propellers turning. The propellers and the nose-wheel are plastic. Unlike some of the other models shown on this spread, the wing section is not detachable. Length: 9·75in (24·765cm); wingspan: 11·5in (29·21cm).

2 Air Transport Service Car Ferry by HWM, West Germany; dating from c1956. This most pleasing tinplate and plastic toy, with the maker's name on one wingtip and the number "S-72" on the other, is in three sections which are fitted together with the aid of spring-clips: a cabin section, with a clear plastic "bubble" loading bay; a wing section; and a twin-boom with tailplane assembly (with red plastic engine nacelles). A friction-drive mechanism in the lower part of the

cabin section drives rubber wheels and produces a siren sound. The plastic bubble opens to allow a toy vehicle (a push-along DUKW of green plastic) to be run in and out. Length: 9·5in (24·13cm); wingspan: 13·5in (34·29cm).

3 Twin-Engined Airliner by Tipp and Company, West Germany; dating from c1956. The finish is almost identical with that of the four-engined airliner by Arnold, shown at (1), but the identification letters differ. This toy is more fully described at (6), *pages 32-33*, where its packaging is shown. Length: 9·75in (24·765cm); wingspan: 12·375in (31·43cm).

4 Passenger Plane by an unidentified maker, People's Republic of China; dating from c1958. This fairly simple tinplate model of a

twin-piston-engined airliner bears the legend "International Express" on the fuselage and has beneath the wing section a paper sticker with "Made in China" in both English and Chinese characters. The upper wing bears the identification "MF 036". A rather clumsy friction motor drives both the rubber wheels and, via a coiled-wire drive, the propellers. The wing section is detachable. Length: 7·125in (18·097cm); wingspan: 9·75in (24·765cm).

5 B.O.A.C. Comet 4 Airliner by Tipp and Company, West Germany; dating from 1958. This is possibly a prototype model rather than a production toy, since it is finished to an unusually high standard: it is apparently hand-painted, with fine detailing of wing panels etc. Friction

drives the main wheels (plastic, with rubber tyres) and produces sparks beneath the clear plastic covers of the engine nacelles. The wing section is detachable. Length: 11·75in (29·845cm); wingspan: 12·25in (31·115cm).

6 Viscount Airliner by Tomy, Japan; dating from c1956. This ingenious toy has a tinplate upper fuselage and tailplane and a plastic lower fuselage and wing section. The plastic engine nacelles have bright metal bands; the propellers are plastic and the main wheels are rubber with metal discs. It is powered by three 1·5-volt batteries in the fuselage forward. The lever on the nose opens the plastic canopy over the cockpit. The levers in front of the plastic half-figures of the pilots are the primary on/off

control (centre) and the controls to start or stop the port and starboard propellers, which revolve with a realistic sound while the wing-lights flash. The nose wheels are steerable, and as the aircraft moves forward the track-mounted figure of a stewardess moves up and down between the rows of moulded plastic passengers. Length: 17·75in (45·085cm); wingspan: 19in (48·26cm).

7 Bristol Bulldog Airplane by Straco, Japan; dating from 1958-59. This toy is fully described at (4), pages 32-33, where it is shown with its original packaging.

8 Training Plane by an unidentified maker, People's Republic of China; dating from c1958. This simple tinplate novelty is clockwork-powered with a permanent winder.

A springloaded lever beneath the fuselage drives the aeroplane along in a series of somersaults. Length: 3·37in (8·57cm); wingspan: 4·125in (10·48cm).

9 Air France Caravelle by Arnold, West Germany; dating from c1959. This fairly simple, but well-made and pleasingly-designed model is tinplate throughout, with rubber tyres on its metal wheels. The maker's trademark and "Made in Germany" are printed on the underside of the fuselage, between the pressed-tin engine nacelles. Friction drives the main wheels. The model was boxed with a fold-out brochure detailing the history and specifications of the aircraft and extolling the virtues of Air France: it was probably intended to be sold primarily at Air

France offices and airport shops. Length: 14·25in (36·195cm); wingspan: 14·5in (36·83cm).

10 Air Plane by an unidentified maker, People's Republic of China; dating from c1958. This cheap and simple friction-driven tinplate toy has two plastic propellers. Length: 6·375in (16·19cm). wingspan: 6·625in (16·83cm).

11 T.W.A. Boeing 727 Jet Airplane by an unidentified Japanese maker; dating from c1961. This large but simple model, rather crude as regards press-work but with much printed detail, is tinplate throughout and has rubber main wheels which are friction-driven. The words "Made in Japan" are stamped below the tailplane on either side. Length: 14·5in (36·83cm); wingspan: 12·25in (31·115cm).

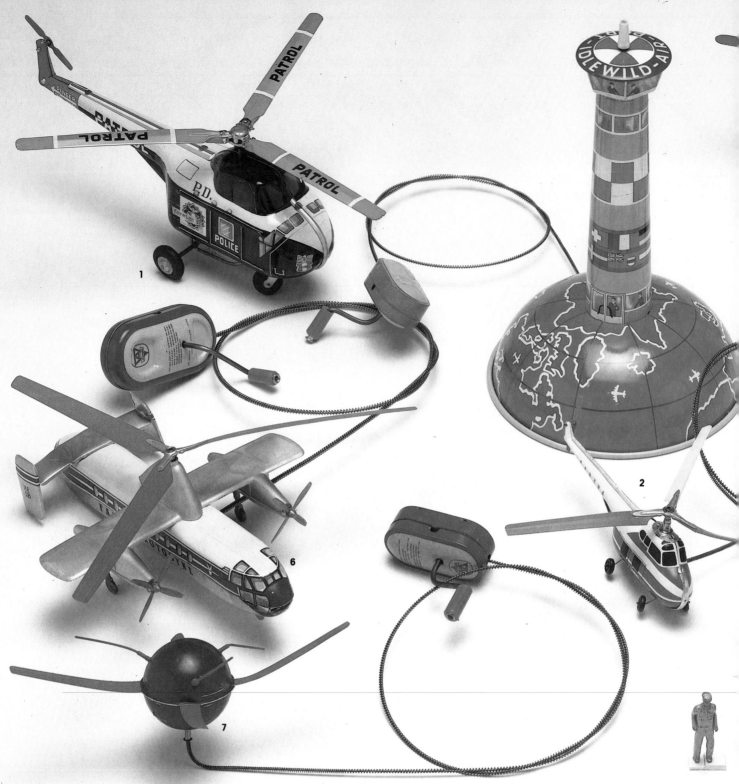

1 Patrol Police Helicopter by an unidentified Japanese maker; dating from *c*1957. Note the applied "Foreign" sticker across the badge on the helicopter's side; the words "Made in Japan" are printed below the "Police" legend on the side away from the camera. The body and main rotor of the toy are tinplate with printed details; the tail rotor is plastic and the cabin is fitted with red plastic windows. The rubber wheels are fitted with metal discs. It is clockwork-powered, with a permanent winder on the side of the undercarriage away from the camera. When it is wound and released, it moves forward with its main rotor (which is removable and may be folded for packaging) turning and the cabin lit up by a sparking mechanism.

The swivel-mounted front wheel of the tricycle undercarriage causes it to steer a quite erratic course. Length: 9·5in (24·13cm); rotor diameter: 11in (27·94cm).
2 Control Tower and Remote-Control Helicopter by Arnold, West Germany; dating from *c*1955. The "Idlewild Airport" tower is of good-quality tinplate, attractively printed with national flags, control room details and, around its base, a world map. The pressed-tin helicopter, with plastic rotor and wheels, is in "Sabena" finish. It is powered by Arnold's own remote-control system, using a manually-cranked handset that transmits power through a cored cable; this is fully described at (5), *pages 32-33.* Details of Arnold's patents are printed on both the handset

and the underside of the tower. The end of the core of the cable running to the helicopter is fitted into the socket on top of the tower, and when the handset is cranked the helicopter takes off and flies most realistically around the tower. Like the other Arnold "flying toys" seen here, it is obviously not suitable for use in a small room! Height of tower: 9in (22·86cm); length of tower-helicopter cable: 27in (68·58cm); length of helicopter:5·5in 913·97cm); rotor diameter: 7in (17·78cm).
3 Helicopter by an unidentified West German maker; dating from *c*1953. The serial number "HK 565" is printed beneath the rotor – see also (4) – and the words "Made in Germany" are printed on the side of the fuselage

away from the camera. This simple, colourfully-printed tinplate toy is clockwork-powered (note the winding shaft just forward of the large rubber main wheels); the folding rotor blades are plastic, as is the small rear wheel. Length: 10·25in (26·035cm); rotor diameter: 9·625in (24·48cm).
4 Helicopter by an unidentified West German maker; dating from *c*1959. Bearing the serial number "HK-570", this simple toy of tab-and-slot construction is obviously by the same maker and of the same period as (4). Its folding blades are metal and its wheels are plastic. It is friction-driven. Length: 7·75in (19·685cm); rotor diameter: 7in (17·78cm).
5 Astra Copter by an unidentified Japanese maker; dating from

c1959. Tinplate throughout, save for the clear plastic tail rotor (with "spinning" markings), this was one of the earlier Japanese tinplate toys made specifically for export. It bears US Navy markings, and is battery-powered with bump-and-go action. The mechanism incorporates an intermittent stop: when this operates, the side hatch opens; see *Inset*. The red plastic light mounted atop the rotor flashes while the toy is in motion.
Length: 12in (30·48cm); rotor diameter: 15·5in (39·37cm).

6 Remote-Control Helibus by Arnold, West Germany; dating from c1956. Since this is a "flying" model using Arnold's remote-control system, the body of the helibus is made of very lightweight tinplate; the wing and tail sections, propellers, rotors

and wheels are plastic. The legend "Fairey Autodyne' is printed along the sides. Length: 8·5in (21·59cm); rotor diameter: 11in (27·94cm); control cable: 32in (81·28cm).

7 Remote-Control Satellite by Arnold, West Germany; dating from late 1957. This fascinating toy is fully described at (5), *pages 32-33,* where its packaging is shown. Vane diameter: 6·75in (17·145cm); control cable: 31in (78·74cm).

8 Remote-Control Piccolo Helicopter by Arnold, West Germany; dating from c1954. In blue-and-white "Sabena" printed livery, this lightweight tinplate toy is another of Arnold's "flying" models powered by a remote-control handset. As the speed of the hand-cranking is increased, the helicopter takes off from the ground; it can be made to

change course, climb or dive by altering the angle at which the handset is held — and can be made to fly backwards by cranking in reverse! The pitch of the rotor blades can also be altered, to improve lifting power, by twisting around the metal sockets of the plastic vanes with pliers.
Length: 5·5in (13·97cm); rotor diameter: 7in (17·78cm); length of control cable: 31in (78·74cm).

9 Helicopter by Biller, West Germany; dating from 1958-59. This is a quite fascinating novelty toy of printed tinplate. Both the helicopter itself, with plastic rotor, and its landing base are clockwork-powered. When both are wound, the helicopter is placed on the "Start" section of the base. When the speed-control lever on

the "Start" side, at the end of the base, is moved forward, the helicopter takes off, its rotor turning, and flies on its wire supporting arm around the globe-mounted "radar dish", its movement registering on the plastic-shielded screen between the control levers. The lever on the "Landing" side of the base controls the height.
Length of helicopter: 3·75in (9·525cm); rotor diameter: 4·25in (10·795cm); length of base: 9·75in (24·765cm).

Inset (above): *Closeup detail of the side of the Japanese-made Astra Copter shown at (4). When the intermittent "stop" mechanism operates, the side hatch springs open and the printed pressed-tin astronaut waves his jointed arm.*

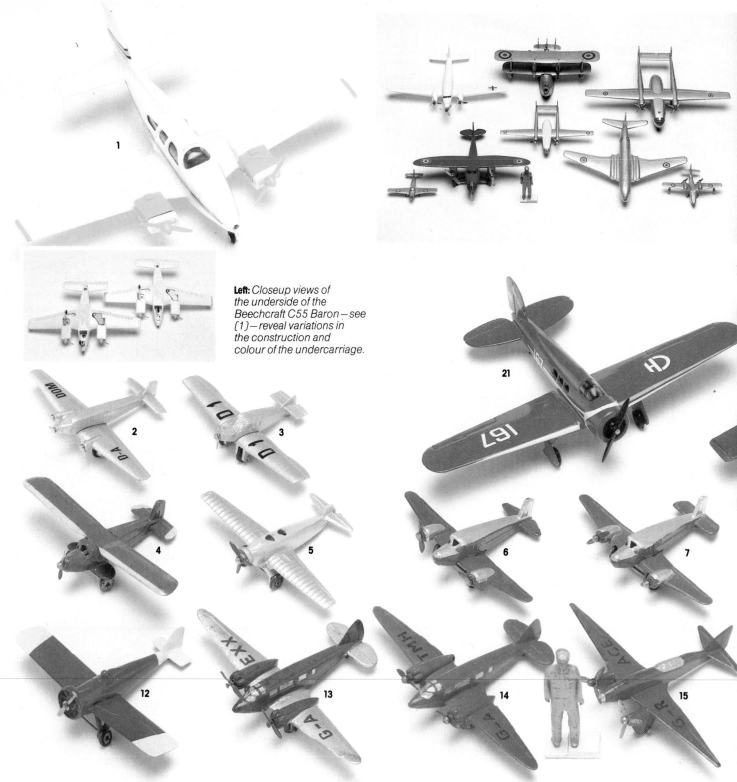

Left: *Closeup views of the underside of the Beechcraft C55 Baron — see (1) — reveal variations in the construction and colour of the undercarriage.*

1 Beechcraft C55 Baron by Dinky Toys, Great Britain; Dinky Toys Reference Number (DT No) 715, in production 1968-76. This model, featuring detachable engine covers and a retractable undercarriage, appeared also in military green finish as the US Army T.42A (DT No 712, 1972-77). A common item. Wingspan: 5·8125in (148mm).

2 Junkers Ju 52 Airliner by Schuco, West Germany; maker's reference number (MRN) 335784, dating from around 1970. It has metal wheels that are fitted with rubber tyres. Wingspan: 2·875in (73mm).

3 Junkers F13 Monoplane by Schuco, West Germany; MRN 335779, dating from around 1970. It has metal wheels that, as at (2), are fitted with rubber tyres. Wingspan: 2·75in (70mm).

4 Henriot H 180T by Dinky Toys, France; French Dinky Toys Reference Number (FDT No) 60c, in production around 1935-40. Wingspan: 3·15in (80mm).

5 Farman F360; FDT No 61c, in production 1938-40. A limited item. Wingspan: 2·75in (70mm).

6-7 Potez 56; FDT No 61b, in production c1938-40. The two versions shown illustrate colour and casting variants: (6) has a tapered tailplane, while the tailplane of (7) is squared off. Wingspan: 2·75in (70mm).

8 Dewoitine 500; FDT No 60e, in production 1935-40. A limited item. Wingspan: 3·15in (80mm).

9 Potez 58; FDT No 60b, in production 1935-40. The example shown has been repainted. Wingspan: 2·99in (76mm).

10 Bréguet Corsaire; FDT No 60d, in production from 1935 until 1940. Wingspan: 3·125in (79mm).

11 General Monospar Plane; DT No 60e. The version shown, in silver, was in production 1936-40. It was made also in gold-and-red finish in 1934-36. Limited availability. Wingspan: 3·15in (80mm).

12 Low Wing Monoplane; DT No 60d. This aircraft was made in red-and-cream, without pilot, in 1934-36, and appeared in orange, with pilot and registration letters "G-A VYP", in 1936-40. The aircraft shown appears to be a repainted later version. A limited item. Wingspan: 3·03in (77mm).

13 King's Aeroplane (Airspeed Envoy); DT No 62k, in production 1938-41. Limited. Wingspan: 3·62in (92mm).

14 Airspeed Envoy Monoplane; DT No 62m, in production 1938-41. The same casting as (20), but easier to find in this finish. Wingspan: 3·62in (92mm).

15 Light Racer (D.H. Comet); DT No 60g. This model appeared in this and other finishes with the letters "G-R ACE" in 1946-49. It was made in red-and-gold in 1935-37, and in silver in 1937-40. All versions are limited. Wingspan: 3·375in (86mm).

16 Percival Gull (Amy Mollinson's); DT No 60k. The model appeared as seen here, in blue-and-silver with the letters "G-A DZO" in blue, in 1936. It was marketed in a special box commemorating Amy Mollinson's record-breaking flight to Capetown and back. It appeared in the same finish, but with "G-A DZO" in black, in

1937-40, to mark H.L. Brook's South African flight. See also (17) and (18). Both versions are limited. Wingspan: 2·99in (76mm).

17 Percival Gull Light Tourer; DT No 60k, the post-War reissue of (16) and (18), appearing in single-colour finishes in 1946-48. Fairly common.

18 Percival Gull; DT No 60c. The first version of this aircraft, appearing in white-and-blue in 1934-37. It was made in single-colour finishes with the letters "G-A DZO" in 1937-40. Easier to find than (16).

19 D.H. Leopard Moth; DT No 60b. This was made in various finishes in 1934-36, and in silver only in 1936-40. The earlier versions are rarer. Wingspan: 2·99in (76mm).

20 Messerschmitt Me 108 Noregrin (in civil livery) by CIJ, France. Wingspan: 2·375in (60mm).

21 Lockheed Orion by NZG, West Germany; dating from around 1965. This large, well-detailed model is fitted with plastic windows, wheels and propeller. Wingspan: 5·25in (133mm).

22-23 Beechcraft Bonanza S35; DT No 710, in production 1965-76. Two colour finishes are shown. This is a quite common item. Wingspan: 5·0625in (129mm).

24 Hawker Siddeley HS 125; DT No 723, in production 1970-75. It has a retractable undercarriage. It is easily available. Wingspan: 5·1875in (132mm).

25 Lear Jet 25B by Schuco, West Germany; MRN 335794, dating from around 1960. It has metal wheels that are fitted with rubber tyres. Wingspan: 2·0625in (52mm).

26 Sikorsky S58 Helicopter; FDT No 60D, issued in May 1957, renumbered 802 in 1959, in production until 1961. Limited. Fuselage length: 3·15in (80mm); rotor diameter: 3·44in (87mm).

27 Sikorsky Float Helicopter by Solido, France; c1960. Limited. Fuselage length: 3in (76mm); rotor diameter: 3·3125in (84mm).

28 Bell Police Helicopter; DT No 732, in production 1974-80. It was also made in "Police Crash Squad" (DT No 299) and "Commando Squad" (DT No 303) versions. It is a common item. Fuselage length: 8·307in (211mm).

29 Bristol 173 Helicopter; DT No 715 — note that it bears the same number as the Beechcraft C55 Baron at (1) — in production 1956-62. A fairly common model. Fuselage length: 5·00in (127mm).

30 Westland Sikorsky S51 Helicopter; DT No 716, in production 1957-62. Fuselage length: 3·504in (89mm).

31 Cierva Autogiro; DT No 60f, in production 1934-41. It appeared also in camouflage finish (DT No 66f; 1940-41). Limited availability. Fuselage length: 2·008in (51mm).

Inset (top left): *(Back row) Fiat G212 Tri-Motor by Mercury, Italy; "Singapore" Flying Boat, DT No 60h, 1936-40; SNCAN Noratlas, FDT No 804, first issued 1960. (Centre) SNCAN Noratlas by CIJ, France. (Front row) Messerschmitt Me 108 Noregrin by CIJ, France; Tri-Motor High-Wing Monoplane by an unidentified French maker; Comet 4 Airliner by Lone Star, Great Britain; Piaggio 136 Seaplane by Mercury, Italy.*

1 Shetland Flying Boat by Dinky Toys, Great Britain; Dinky Toys Reference Number (DT No) 701. This model was first issued in 1947 and remained in production until 1949. The example shown has been repainted: the model originally bore the registration letters "G-A GVD" and "BX". A fairly scarce item. Wingspan: 9·25in (235mm).

2 Empire Flying Boat; DT No 60r, first issued in 1937, in production until 1940, and reissued after World War II. This model appeared with fifteen different sets of registration letters and names: the letters "G-A DHM" on the example shown mark it as the "Caledonia", first of the series. See also (5). This example has been refitted with four-bladed propellers; as seen at (5), three-bladed propellers were

originally fitted. A limited item. Wingspan: 6·18in (157mm).

3 Mayo Composite Aircraft; DT No 63, first issued in 1939 and in production until 1941. These two aircraft were issued both in composite form, as seen here, and as separate items. The composite model is by far the hardest to find and may be described as fairly scarce. Wingspans: (upper) 3·976in (101mm); (lower) 6·18in (157mm).

4 Seaplane "Mercury"; DT No 63b. The upper component of the Mayo Composite shown at (3); this was available as a separate item in 1939-41, and again after World War II until 1954. A limited item. Wingspan: 3·976in (101mm).

5 Empire Flying Boat; DT No 60r. This version of the model described at (2) is fitted with propellers of the

original type. The letters "G-A DUV" mark it as the version named "Cambria". A limited item. Wingspan: 6·18in (157mm).

6 Flying Boat "Clipper III"; DT No 60w, first issued in 1938-40 and available post-War from 1946 until 1948. This example has been repainted: it was issued by the maker in silver only. The pre-War version, which bears registration letters, will be fairly hard to find. Wingspan: 6·46in (164mm).

7-8 Armstrong Whitworth Air Liner; DT No 62p. As seen at (7), in silver finish, this model first appeared in 1938 and until 1941 was available with six different letterings and names: this example has the letters "G-A DSV", marking it as "Explorer". It was reissued in 1946-49, when it was available

either in silver or in two-tone finish as seen at (8). Neither version will now be particularly hard to find. Wingspan: 6·81in (173mm).

9-10 Vickers Viking Airliner; DT No 70c, first issued in 1947, later renumbered 705, and in production until 1962. Earlier versions, as seen at (9), are finished in silver; later ones, as seen at (10), in grey. Both versions bear the letters "G-A GOL", and neither is hard to find. Wingspan: 5·51in (140mm).

11 Four-engined Air Liner; DT No 60r, first issued in 1946 and in production until 1949. See also (20). The model was originally available, with the same number, as the D.H. Albatross Mail Liner, in 1939-41. The pre-War version bore the letters "G-A EVV". Neither version is hard to find, but the

pre-War aeroplane is the rarer. Wingspan: 5·7in (145mm).

12 Dewoitine D338 Tri-Motor by Dinky Toys, France; French Dinky Toys Reference Number (FDT No) 61a, first issued in 1938 and available until 1940. Limited. Wingspan: 5·275in (134mm).

13 Lockheed Super 6 Constellation; FDT No 60c. This model in "Air France" livery was first issued in 1959 and was in production until 1962. It is a limited item. Wingspan: 7·87in (200mm).

14 Bristol Britannia; DT No 998, first issued in 1959 and in production until 1965. It appeared only in "Canadian Pacific" livery, as shown; but see (18) for a colour variation. This is a limited item. Wingspan: 8·86in (225mm).

15 Vickers Viscount Airliner; DT No 708, first issued in 1957 and in production until 1965. In "British European Airways" livery, this example is finished in silver, white and red; in some later production models, silver is replaced by grey. It is of limited availability. Wingspan: 5·87in (149mm).

16 Vickers Viscount Airliner; DT No 706, first issued in 1956 and in production until 1957. This is in "Air France" finish but otherwise resembles (15). It was produced for only a short time and may be hard to find. Wingspan: 5·87in (149mm).

17 Douglas DC3; DT No 60t, first issued in 1938 and in production until 1940. Note the small hole in the centre of the fuselage, provided for what a leaflet packed by Dinky Toys with many of its pre-War aeroplanes called "Gliding". A

string was passed through the looped top of a split-pin inserted into the hole; with the string suitably secured at both ends the model could be glided, with the aid of another string fixed to its tail, to a stable landing. Only models made up to early 1940 have the "gliding hole". It is a limited item. Wingspan: 5·197in (132mm).

18 Bristol Britannia; DT No 998. As (14) in all respects save one: a blue stripe replaces the red stripe on the sides and tailfin.

19 Vickers Viscount Airliner; this appears to be DT No 708 — see (15) — but is a "Nicky Toy", made in India from obsolete dies sold by Meccano c1968-70.

20 Four-Engined Air Liner; DT No 62r. This is a colour variation of the model shown at (11).

21 Avro York Airliner; DT No 70a, first issued in 1946, later renumbered 704, and in production until 1959. it is a fairly common model. Wingspan: 6·29in (160mm).

22 Junkers Ju90 Airliner; DT No 62n, first issued in 1939 and in production until 1941. Note the "gliding hole". See also (23). Fairly scarce. Wingspan: 6·22in (158mm).

23 Giant High Speed Monoplane; DT No 62y, first issued in 1946 and in production until 1949. It is a fairly easily available model. Wingspan: 6·22in (158mm).

24 Vickers Viscount Airliner; FDT No 60e, first issued in 1959, later renumbered 803, and in production until 1961. Compare this model with the version by Dinky Toys, Great Britain, at (16). Scarce. Wingspan: 5·87in (149mm).

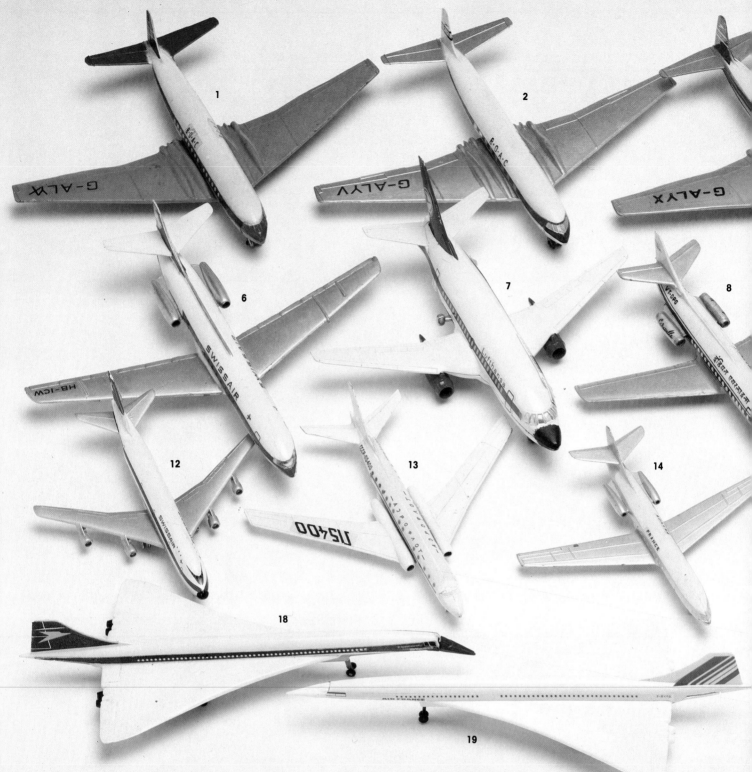

1 DH Comet Jet Airliner by Dinky Toys, Great Britain; Dinky Toys Reference Number (DT No) 999. In "B.O.A.C." (British Overseas Airways Corporation) livery, this model of the first jet airliner to enter commercial service was first issued in 1954 as DT No 702; see (2). This example was produced after c1964, by which time renumbering had taken place, the silver finish of the original had given way to metallic grey, and the registration letters "G-ALYX" were carried. The model was in production until 1965. Limited. Wingspan: 7·24in (184mm).

2 DH Comet Jet Airliner; DT No 702. In comparison with (1), note the silver finish and the registration letters "G-ALYV". A limited item. Wingspan: as (1).

3 DH Comet Jet Airliner by Nicky Toys, India. Although this is near-identical with (1) and (2), it is a model produced in India from Dinky Toys dies that had been sold as obsolete by Meccano in the 1960s. Note that the finish differs from (1) and (2); there are fewer cabin windows. Wingspan: as (1).

4 Caravelle SE 210 by Dinky Toys, Great Britain; DT No 997, issued in 1962 and in production until 1965. Compare the finish of this model of Sud Aviation's twin-engined airliner, in "Air France" livery, to that of the original version by French Dinky Supertoys, shown at (5). Limited. Wingspan: 7·09in (180mm).

5 Caravelle SE 210 by Dinky Toys, France; French Dinky Toys Reference Number (FDT No) 60f, issued in 1959, later renumbered 891, and in production until 1968. This was the original version of the model: the British version shown at (4) was made with French tooling. Note that this has the registration letters differently arranged. Limited. Wingspan: as (4).

6 Caravelle SE 210 by Tekno, Denmark; dating from the 1960s. In "Swissair" livery, this model features a retractable undercarriage. Wingspan: 6·625in (168mm).

7 Boeing 737 by Dinky Toys, Great Britain; DT No 717, issued in 1970 and in production until 1975. In "Lufthansa" livery, this example has blue engine pods, which mark it as a later production model; earlier models had white pods. The lever that operates its retractable undercarriage—it was the first Dinky Toys aircraft thus equipped

—is visible just behind the starboard wing. It is a fairly common item. Wingspan: 6in (152mm).

8 Caravelle Airliner by Milton, Great Britain; dating from the 1960s. In the livery of a Middle Eastern airline, with Arabic lettering, this model is fitted with plastic wheels. Wingspan: 5in (127mm).

9 DH 106 Comet Airliner by CIJ, France; maker' reference number (MRN) 407, dating from the 1960s. It is in "B.O.A.C." livery and bears the registration letters "G-BOAC". Wingspan: 5·4375in (138mm).

10 Douglas DC-7 Airliner by CIJ, France; dating from the 1960s. Note the plated spinners; see also (15). Wingspan: 4·625in (117mm).

11 Boeing 707 Airliner by CIJ, France; dating from the 1960s. In "Air France" livery, this model is made

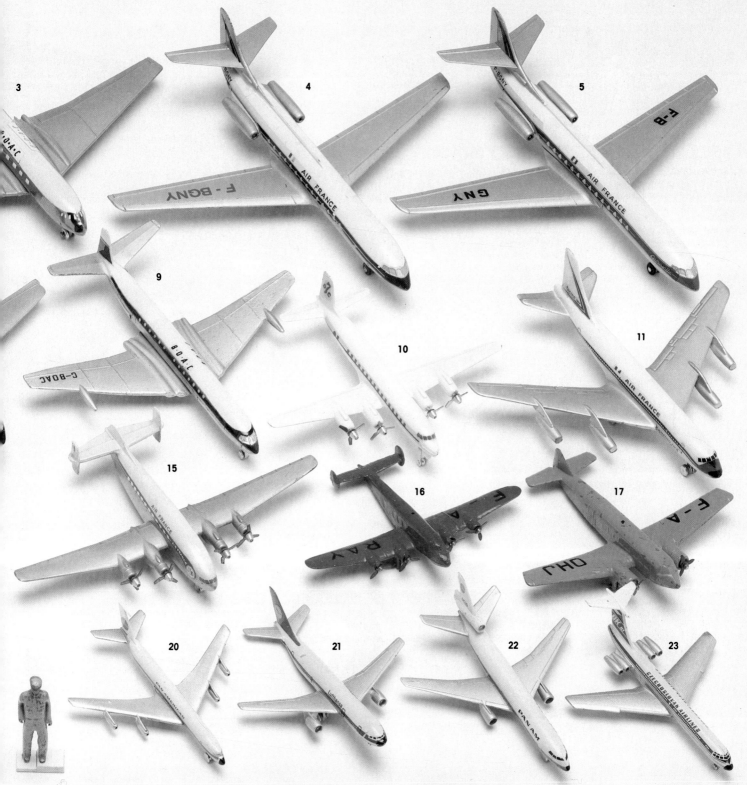

to scale of around 1:300. Wingspan: 5·3125in (135mm).

12 Boeing 747B Airliner by Schuco, West Germany; MRN 335 793, dating from around 1975. In Swissair" livery, this model is fitted with metal undercarriage wheels. Wingspan: 3·875in (98mm).

13 Tupolev Tu 104 Airliner by Solido, France; dating from around 1970. This model of a Soviet airliner is in "Aeroflot" livery, complete with the correct Cyrillic (Russian) lettering. Wingspan: 4·1825in (122mm).

14 Caravelle Airliner by CIJ, France; dating from the 1960s. This is a small and simple model in comparison with the versions by Dinky Toys of Great Britain (4) and France (5), and Tekno of Denmark (6). Wingspan: 4·5in (114mm).

15 Bréguet Deux Ponts Airliner by

CIJ, France; MRN 763, dating from the 1960s. This nicely-finished model is in "Air France" livery. Like (10), it is fitted with plated spinners. Wingspan: 5·6875in (144mm).

16 Potez 662 Airliner by Dinky Toys, France; FDT No 64d, issued in 1939 and in production until 1940. It incorporates a "gliding hole" — see note at (17), *pages 120-121* — in the centre of the fuselage. Limited. Wingspan: 4·055in (103mm).

17 Bloch 220 Airliner by Dinky Toys, France; FDT No 64b, first issued in 1939, reissued after World War II, and in production until 1948. Like (16), it has a "gliding hole". Limited. Wingspan: 4·094in (104mm).

18 Aérospatiale/BAC Concorde Airliner by Corgi Toys, Great Britain; dating from around 1969. This well-finished model

incorporates the adjustable nose (here shown in the "droop" position) of the prototype. However, Corgi's desire to be up-to-date with this model outran reality: it is in "B.O.A.C." livery, but by the time Concorde entered service early in 1976, B.O.A.C. had given way to British Airways: Concorde never flew in B.O.A.C. livery. Fairly common. Wingspan: 3·3125in (84mm).

19 Aérospatiale/BAC Concorde Airliner by Corgi Toys; the companion to (18), in "Air France" livery and with the nose shown in the raised position. The registration letters, "F-BVFA", are those used by Air France on its first Concorde. This is a fairly common item. Wingspan: as (18).

20 Boeing 707 Airliner by Schuco, West Germany; MRN 335 787,

dating from around 1970. This model is in "Pan American" livery and, like the similar small-scale models by Schuco shown at (21), (22) and (23), it is fitted with metal wheels. Wingspan: 3in (76mm).

21 Airbus A300B by Schuco, West Germany; MRN 335 795, dating from the 1970s. It is in "Lufthansa" livery. Wingspan: 3in (76mm).

22 McDonnell Douglas DC-10 Airliner by Schuco, West Germany; MRN 335 792, dating from the 1970s. This model is in "Pan American" livery. Wingspan: 3·0625in (78mm).

23 Ilyushin Il-62 Airliner by Schuco, West Germany; MRN 335 797, dating from around 1974. This model of a Soviet-built airliner is in "Czechoslovakian Airlines" livery. and has a well-detailed finish. Wingspan: 2·8125in (71mm).

Pedal-Powered Vehicles by British Makers, 1930s-1950s

Right: *Big Tip Lorry by Tri-ang (Lines Brothers Limited), Great Britain; dating from around 1930. This impressive pedal-powered vehicle is shown in partly-restored condition: it awaits the provision of an adjustable windscreen, an upholstered seat and direction indicators, as specified in Tri-ang's catalogue description. Its restored paintwork incorporates the name of "Shaun Magee's Pedal Car Museum", the major collection at Bishop's Waltham, Hampshire, on which we were allowed to draw for the pedal vehicles shown on this spread. The lorry is of mainly wooden construction, with a radiator, louvred bonnet, mudguards and step plates of sheet metal. It is treadle-operated, with drive to one wheel via a cranked ball-bearing rear axle. Simple Ackerman steering is fitted, with a four-spoked chromed steering wheel. The tipping rear body, which is fitted with a hinged tailboard, is operated by a side-mounted lever. Other details include imitation headlights and sidelights and a dashboard with printed instrumentation. It is fitted with 11in (28cm) balloon-disc wheels with ⅝in (16mm) solid rubber tyres. Length: 61in (155mm).*

Left: *Tri-ang Major Pedal Tractor by Tri-ang, Great Britain; maker's reference number 6014, dating from around 1950. Of all-steel construction, this three-wheeled tractor is treadle-operated, with drive to one wheel via a cranked ball-bearing rear axle. It has a pressed-steel sprung seat and is fitted with mudguards over the rear wheels. The front wheel is a 10in (25cm) balloon disc with a solid rubber tyre and a ball-bearing spindle; the rear wheels are 11½in (29cm) balloon discs with ½in (13mm) rubber tyres. Length: 35in (89cm).*

Left: *Tipping Lorry by Leeway, Great Britain; dating from 1954. Of wood and metal construction, this vehicle is fitted with Leeway's typical and very distinctive radiator of pressed steel; the louvred bonnet is of the same material. The chassis is wooden, as is the lever-operated tipping rear body with its hinged tailboard. The raised seat, with back support, is upholstered, and the four-spoked metal steering wheel operates simple Ackerman steering. It is powered by treadle drive to a cranked rear axle. The pressed-steel disc wheels are fitted with ½in (13mm) rubber tyres. This toy is in unrestored condition and is without the windscreen that was originally fitted: it is of course, quite unusual to find pedal-powered toys in anything other than "play-worn" condition and in need of restoration. Length: 46in (117cm).*

Left: *Police Jeep by Tri-ang, Great Britain; dating from c1958. The Jeep was perhaps the most famous vehicle to be developed during World War II, when approximately 64,000 were made, and in the immediate post-War period there can have been few small boys who did not wish to own a toy modelled on it. Tri-ang responded first with a small clockwork model in the "Minic" range, see pages 40-41, 42-43, and then with a pedal-powered vehicle. The pedal Jeep was first made in military finish, in olive-drab with the Allied "Invasion Star" on the bonnet. The example shown here, however, is Tri-ang's Police Jeep: in the earlier post-War period, when four-wheel-drive high-mobility vehicles were not otherwise generally available, many Jeeps found their way into Police service. This toy is of pressed-steel construction, with a fold-down windscreen (frame only). The example shown is in unrestored condition, lacking the spare wheel and jerrican originally fitted. Children who expected the toy to perform like its prototype will have been disappointed, for only a single wheel, with a smooth tyre, is driven by the adjustable treadle action, working via a cranked rear axle. The pressed-steel balloon-disc wheels (with hubcaps missing from this example) are fitted with narrow tyres of smooth rubber. The three-spoked plastic steering wheel on this example is of a late type: a four-spoked steering wheel was more often fitted. Length: 37in (94cm).*

126

127